JUMBLE®

Explosion

A Puzzle Boom!

Henri Arnold,
Bob Lee,
and
Mike Argirion

TRIUMPH
BOOKS

This book is available in quantity at special discounts
for your group or organization.

For further information, contact:

Triumph Books
542 South Dearborn Street
Suite 750
Chicago, Illinois 60605
(312) 939-3330
Fax (312) 663-3557

Printed in U.S.A.

ISBN: 978-1-60078-078-3

Design by Sue Knopf

CONTENTS

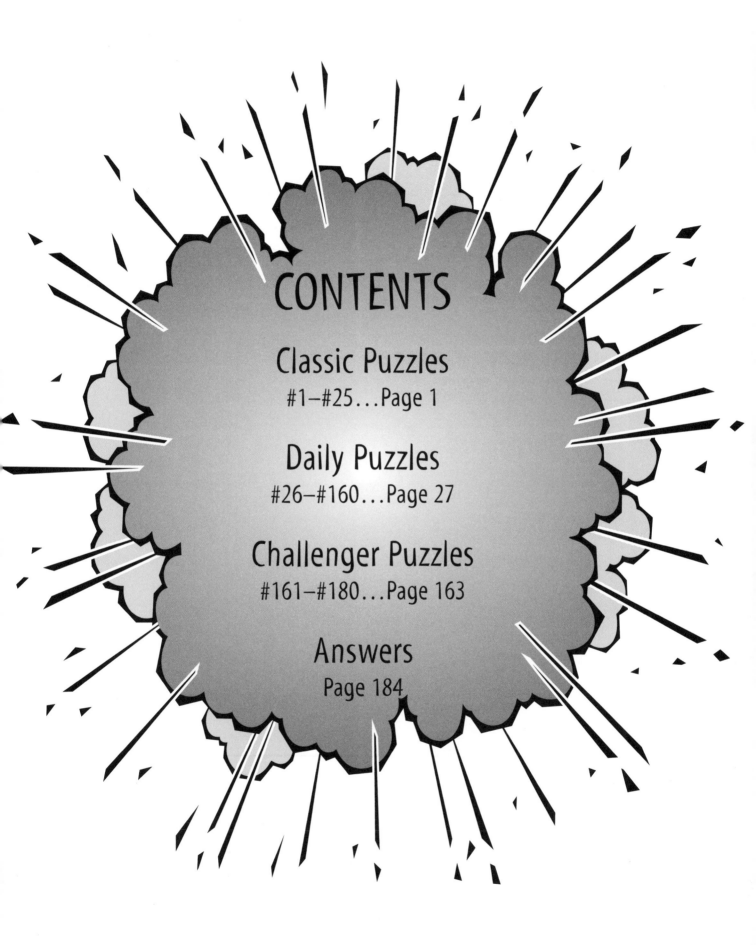

JUMBLE®

Explosion

CLASSIC PUZZLES

JUMBLE®

Unscramble these four Jumbles, one letter to each square, to form four ordinary words.

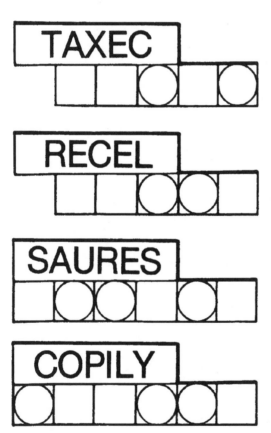

TAXEC

RECEL

SAURES

COPILY

THE MOST BRUTAL PART OF THAT HEAVYWEIGHT FIGHT.

Now arrange the circled letters to form the surprise answer, as suggested by the above cartoon.

Print answer here THE ______ OF THE ______

PUZZLE 2

JUMBLE®

Unscramble these four Jumbles, one letter to each square, to form four ordinary words.

NEPEC

LIVIG

TIGBLE

OVVEEL

You were right all along, dear
THE HARDEST THING TO GIVE IS---

Now arrange the circled letters to form the surprise answer, as suggested by the above cartoon.

Print answer here

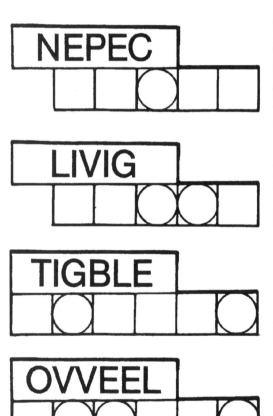

JUMBLE®

Unscramble these four Jumbles, one letter to each square, to form four ordinary words.

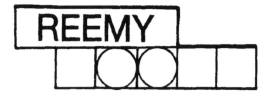

DAGEA

REEMY

PEESLY

RUSTEM

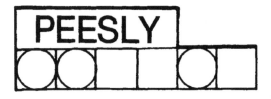

WHAT THAT WILD-ANIMAL TRAINER AT THE CIRCUS DOES.

Now arrange the circled letters to form the surprise answer, as suggested by the above cartoon.

Print answer here " " TO

PUZZLE 4

JUMBLE®

Unscramble these four Jumbles, one letter to each square, to form four ordinary words.

LITEE

GEDEH

WALLUF

HARTTO

Cheer up -- there are a lot more fish in the sea
I am breaking off our engagement because...
THAT LETTER MADE ILL WILL.

Now arrange the circled letters to form the surprise answer, as suggested by the above cartoon.

Print answer here ◯◯◯ ◯◯◯◯◯◯ "◯"

PUZZLE 5

JUMBLE®

Unscramble these four Jumbles, one letter to each square, to form four ordinary words.

YOWNS

GEBOF

SMEECH

HIRSLE

Don't worry -- I'll drive
COCKTAIL LOUNGE
WHAT HORSEPOWER SHOULD BE MIXED WITH.

Now arrange the circled letters to form the surprise answer, as suggested by the above cartoon.

Print answer here

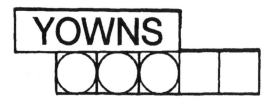

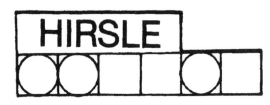

PUZZLE 6

JUMBLE®

Unscramble these four Jumbles, one letter to each square, to form four ordinary words.

MUIBE

LOFAR

SLEAWE

DULBOY

There've been some changes since I was last here
WHAT THOSE NEWLY HATCHED TERMITES WERE.

Now arrange the circled letters to form the surprise answer, as suggested by the above cartoon.

Print answer here ☐☐☐☐☐ IN THE ☐☐☐☐☐

PUZZLE 7

JUMBLE®

Unscramble these four Jumbles, one letter to each square, to form four ordinary words.

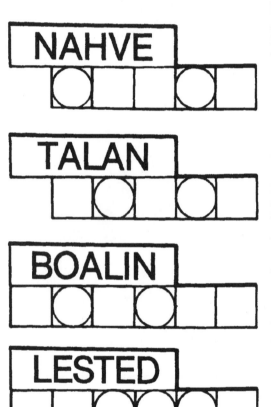

NAHVE

TALAN

BOALIN

LESTED

THAT UNCONVINCING WITNESS WAS MAKING THE JURY WONDER---

Now arrange the circled letters to form the surprise answer, as suggested by the above cartoon.

Print answer here WHAT "   "

JUMBLE®

Unscramble these four Jumbles, one letter to each square, to form four ordinary words.

PLEEO

BELLI

LIFTLE

ENTAUB

WHAT YOU WOULDN'T EXPECT A VEGETARIAN TO DO WHEN THE FOOD IS UNSATISFACTORY.

Now arrange the circled letters to form the surprise answer, as suggested by the above cartoon.

Print answer here ________ ________ IT

PUZZLE 9

JUMBLE®

Unscramble these four Jumbles, one letter to each square, to form four ordinary words.

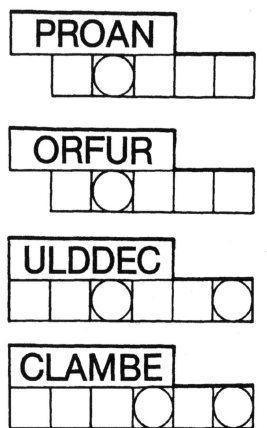

PROAN

ORFUR

ULDDEC

CLAMBE

WHAT THAT QUARRELING ACTING TEAM ALWAYS DID JUST BEFORE GOING ON STAGE.

Now arrange the circled letters to form the surprise answer, as suggested by the above cartoon.

Print answer here " "

PUZZLE 10

JUMBLE®

Unscramble these four Jumbles, one letter to each square, to form four ordinary words.

VARFO

NISOB

LOWHYL

GUMMAN

WHAT THAT BASHFUL WALLFLOWER WAS HOPING TO DO WITH THE MAN OF HER CHOICE.

Now arrange the circled letters to form the surprise answer, as suggested by the above cartoon.

Print answer here

JUMBLE®

Unscramble these four Jumbles, one letter to each square, to form four ordinary words.

TALEE

VICLI

MUTTUL

TANIED

—COMING SOON!
WHAT A SIESTA IS.

Now arrange the circled letters to form the surprise answer, as suggested by the above cartoon.

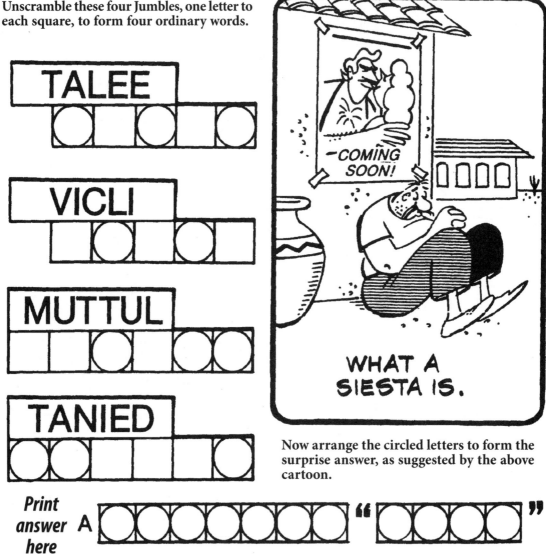

Print answer here A ________ "_____"

PUZZLE 12

JUMBLE®

Unscramble these four Jumbles, one letter to each square, to form four ordinary words.

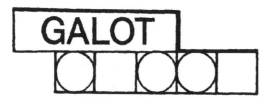

UMPIO

GALOT

HYNDIG

BLATOC

He didn't put a penny in it
It takes money to make money
SHOES

A GUY WHO TRIES TO START A BUSI-NESS ON A SHOE-STRING SOMETIMES ENDS UP TAKING THIS.

Now arrange the circled letters to form the surprise answer, as suggested by the above cartoon.

Print answer here A "   "

PUZZLE 13

JUMBLE®

Unscramble these four Jumbles, one letter to each square, to form four ordinary words.

AVERB

RESEA

DAUPIN

YUCLOD

WHEN YOU CALL THE PLUMBER BECAUSE OF A LEAK, IT MIGHT END UP BEING THIS.

Now arrange the circled letters to form the surprise answer, as suggested by the above cartoon.

Print answer here A “ ” ON

PUZZLE 14

JUMBLE®

Unscramble these four Jumbles, one letter to each square, to form four ordinary words.

YENED

BROAN

DEECES

SLETED

How beautiful
I wouldn't be too sure

THE JUDGE'S WORDS WERE LESS IMPORTANT THAN THIS.

Now arrange the circled letters to form the surprise answer, as suggested by the above cartoon.

Print answer here HIS

JUMBLE®

Unscramble these four Jumbles, one letter to each square, to form four ordinary words.

VERPO

HEEPS

FUNIES

CIAMAN

He'll go far
WHAT AN EMPLOYEE HAS IF HE LAUGHS AT THE BOSS'S JOKES EVEN WHEN THEY MAKE NO THIS.

Now arrange the circled letters to form the surprise answer, as suggested by the above cartoon.

Print answer here " "

PUZZLE 16

JUMBLE®

Unscramble these four Jumbles, one letter to each square, to form four ordinary words.

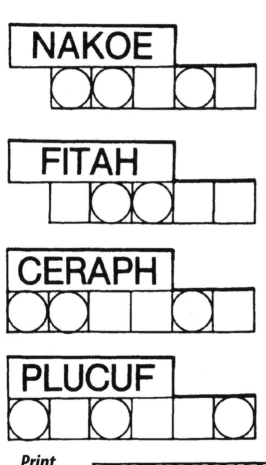

COULD BE A HEAD COVERING FOR A TRAVELER TO THE ARCTIC.

NAKOE

FITAH

CERAPH

PLUCUF

Now arrange the circled letters to form the surprise answer, as suggested by the above cartoon.

Print answer here A ______ ____ "___"

JUMBLE®

Unscramble these four Jumbles, one letter to each square, to form four ordinary words.

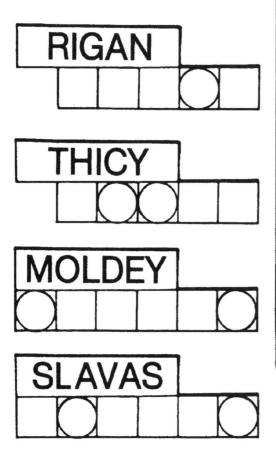

RIGAN

THICY

MOLDEY

SLAVAS

WHAT HAPPENED WHEN THEIR SHELLFISH BUSINESS SUFFERED FINANCIAL REVERSES?

Now arrange the circled letters to form the surprise answer, as suggested by the above cartoon.

Print answer here IT WAS A "◯◯◯◯-◯◯◯"

PUZZLE 18

JUMBLE®

Unscramble these four Jumbles, one letter to each square, to form four ordinary words.

HUMOT

FREVE

SCEPHY

TILPUF

WHAT THE TAXIDERMIST'S PERSONALITY CERTAINLY WAS.

Now arrange the circled letters to form the surprise answer, as suggested by the above cartoon.

Print answer here " "

JUMBLE®

Unscramble these four Jumbles, one letter to each square, to form four ordinary words.

ALTEM

BUTIC

WHADOS

KRILLE

WHAT HE WOULD DO EVERY TIME HE SAW THE GIRL AT THE CANDY COUNTER.

Now arrange the circled letters to form the surprise answer, as suggested by the above cartoon.

Print answer here ☐☐☐☐☐ - ☐☐☐☐ HER

PUZZLE 20

JUMBLE®

Unscramble these four Jumbles, one letter to each square, to form four ordinary words.

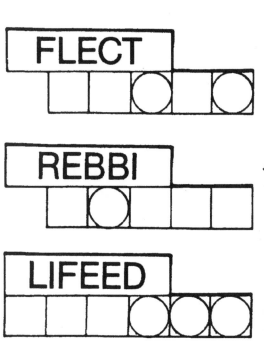

FLECT

REBBI

LIFEED

TACTIN

He's writing to himself
THE EGOTIST'S LOVE LETTER.

Now arrange the circled letters to form the surprise answer, as suggested by the above cartoon.

Print answer here THE ◯◯◯◯◯◯ "◯"

JUMBLE®

Unscramble these four Jumbles, one letter to each square, to form four ordinary words.

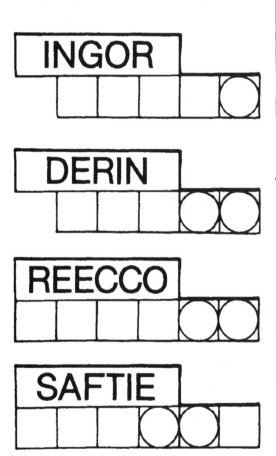

INGOR

DERIN

REECCO

SAFTIE

WHEN THE SKUNK ENTERED THE ROOM, IT GOT ATTENTION BE-CAUSE IT WAS THIS.

Now arrange the circled letters to form the surprise answer, as suggested by the above cartoon.

Print answer here THE " " OF IT

PUZZLE 22

JUMBLE®

Unscramble these four Jumbles, one letter to each square, to form four ordinary words.

MOWNE

NASPY

REOCAN

CREBIK

Must be the weather
TEMPORARILY CLOSED
WHERE THE DEPOSITS ARE "FROZEN ASSETS."

Now arrange the circled letters to form the surprise answer, as suggested by the above cartoon.

Print answer here IN A " "

PUZZLE 23

JUMBLE®

Unscramble these four Jumbles, one letter to each square, to form four ordinary words.

LEETA

NUMIS

SLEPEN

MUDINS

Expect me to wait all day?
THE NERVOUS TAILOR WAS ALWAYS ON THIS.

Now arrange the circled letters to form the surprise answer, as suggested by the above cartoon.

Print answer here &

JUMBLE®

Unscramble these four Jumbles, one letter to each square, to form four ordinary words.

YOVIR

RODIF

THANYS

CAFEED

THAT WELL-DRESSED WOMAN WAS INDEED A CREDIT TO HER HUSBAND, THANKS TO THIS.

Now arrange the circled letters to form the surprise answer, as suggested by the above cartoon.

Print answer here

JUMBLE®

Unscramble these four Jumbles, one letter to each square, to form four ordinary words.

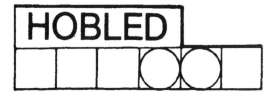

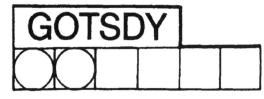

RAMER

MEERY

HOBLED

GOTSDY

It's about time you got some new ones

A COMFORTABLE OLD SHOE MIGHT BE THIS, THROUGH THICK AND THIN.

Now arrange the circled letters to form the surprise answer, as suggested by the above cartoon.

Print answer here YOUR " "

JUMBLE®

Explosion

DAILY PUZZLES

PUZZLE 26

JUMBLE®

Unscramble these four Jumbles, one letter to each square, to form four ordinary words.

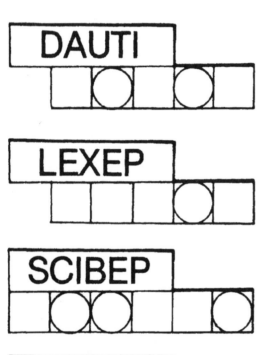

DAUTI

LEXEP

SCIBEP

DUNOAL

WHEN GOSSIP IS AT ITS MOST MALICIOUS, THEY SOMETIMES RELISH IT AS THIS.

Now arrange the circled letters to form the surprise answer, as suggested by the above cartoon.

Print answer here " "

PUZZLE 27

JUMBLE®

Unscramble these four Jumbles, one letter to each square, to form four ordinary words.

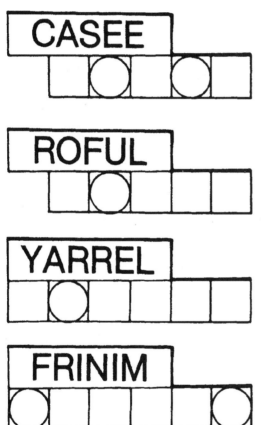

CASEE

ROFUL

YARREL

FRINIM

THE CURVE THAT USUALLY SETS THINGS STRAIGHT.

Now arrange the circled letters to form the surprise answer, as suggested by the above cartoon.

Print answer here

PUZZLE 28

JUMBLE®

Unscramble these four Jumbles, one letter to each square, to form four ordinary words.

GUSET

SULPH

YURSLE

CIRION

His connections didn't help him
WHAT A CROOKED POLITICIAN WITH A "KNOTTY" PROBLEM MIGHT TRY TO DO.

Now arrange the circled letters to form the surprise answer, as suggested by the above cartoon.

Print answer here

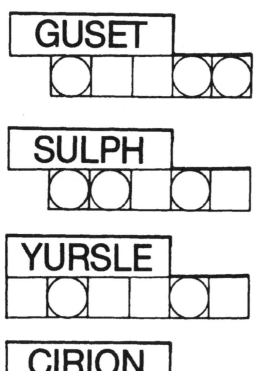

JUMBLE®

Unscramble these four Jumbles, one letter to each square, to form four ordinary words.

OATAR

UBLIT

LAMDAY

TIFELL

WORDS OF PRAISE THAT SELDOM FALL FLAT.

Now arrange the circled letters to form the surprise answer, as suggested by the above cartoon.

Print answer here

JUMBLE®

Unscramble these four Jumbles, one letter to each square, to form four ordinary words.

ERTEX

TEFAC

MOURUQ

PRUINT

We're going to learn how to avoid the mistakes our ancestors made
WHY YOU SHOULD STUDY THE HISTORY OF THE PAST.

Now arrange the circled letters to form the surprise answer, as suggested by the above cartoon.

Print answer here THERE'S A ________ __ IT

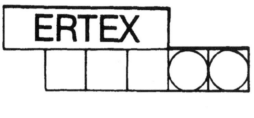

PUZZLE 31

JUMBLE®

Unscramble these four Jumbles, one letter to each square, to form four ordinary words.

GUBEN

DAJED

REWESK

LINCEY

They say he's got a bundle put away

WHAT A GREEN THUMB CAN MEAN FOR A PROFESSIONAL GARDENER.

Now arrange the circled letters to form the surprise answer, as suggested by the above cartoon.

Print answer here " "

JUMBLE®

Unscramble these four Jumbles, one letter to each square, to form four ordinary words.

VUCER

HERBT

ZEEMYN

RAWHOR

WHAT THE MALE SHEEP SHOUTED IN ORDER TO GET HIS MATE'S ATTENTION.

Now arrange the circled letters to form the surprise answer, as suggested by the above cartoon.

Print answer here " , "

PUZZLE 33

JUMBLE®

Unscramble these four Jumbles, one letter to each square, to form four ordinary words.

YUSHK

COAME

FLYJOU

THELAH

WHEN A COWARD GETS INTO A "JAM," YOU CAN EXPECT HIM TO DO THIS.

Now arrange the circled letters to form the surprise answer, as suggested by the above cartoon.

Print answer here ______ LIKE ______

PUZZLE 34

JUMBLE®

Unscramble these four Jumbles, one letter to each square, to form four ordinary words.

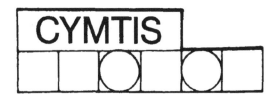

TISOF

PHAMC

SLYGUN

CYMTIS

I say—stay away from all women!
WHAT THE MISOGYNIST FELT HE HAD IN THE WORLD.

Now arrange the circled letters to form the surprise answer, as suggested by the above cartoon.

Print answer here A “ _ _ _ _ - _ _ _ _ ”

PUZZLE 35

JUMBLE®

Unscramble these four Jumbles, one letter to each square, to form four ordinary words.

HASAB

YAHNE

VISWEL

KADMAS

STRONG LUNGS OFTEN APPEAL TO PEOPLE WITH THIS.

Now arrange the circled letters to form the surprise answer, as suggested by the above cartoon.

Print answer here

JUMBLE®

Unscramble these four Jumbles, one letter to each square, to form four ordinary words.

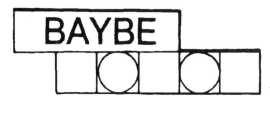

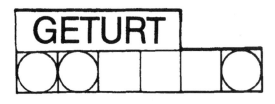

BAYBE

KECHO

LOVEUM

GETURT

Won't be long before we look like them

AGE MAY BE THE DIFFERENCE BETWEEN THESE.

Now arrange the circled letters to form the surprise answer, as suggested by the above cartoon.

Print answer here A ◯◯◯◯◯ & A ◯◯◯◯◯

PUZZLE 37

JUMBLE®

Unscramble these four Jumbles, one letter to each square, to form four ordinary words.

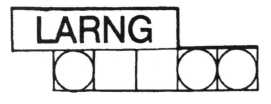

LARNG

NOPER

KIELLY

DEGURT

Opportunity knocked, but he was asleep
A GUY WHO HAS THE RIGHT AIM IN LIFE SOMETIMES FAILS TO DO THIS, FIGURATIVELY.

Now arrange the circled letters to form the surprise answer, as suggested by the above cartoon.

Print answer here "◯◯◯◯ THE ◯◯◯◯◯◯◯"

PUZZLE 38

JUMBLE®

Unscramble these four Jumbles, one letter to each square, to form four ordinary words.

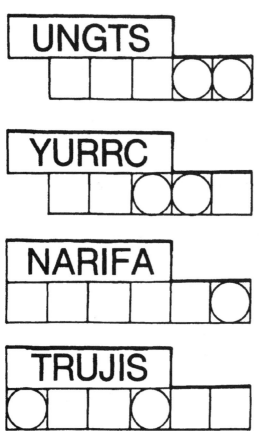

UNGTS

YURRC

NARIFA

TRUJIS

Gee—I'm glad to be out of there

WHAT KIND OF AN EXPERIENCE WAS IT FOR THE JINNI TO BE IN THAT BOTTLE?

Now arrange the circled letters to form the surprise answer, as suggested by the above cartoon.

Print answer here A ☐☐☐☐☐☐☐ ONE

PUZZLE 39

JUMBLE®

Unscramble these four Jumbles, one letter to each square, to form four ordinary words.

KNALB

AWAMC

BAACAN

TRINWY

I know everyone is prepared today
I sure hope so

WHAT THE COLLEGE HALFBACK WAS IN HIS STUDIES.

Now arrange the circled letters to form the surprise answer, as suggested by the above cartoon.

Print answer here

PUZZLE 40

JUMBLE®

Unscramble these four Jumbles, one letter to each square, to form four ordinary words.

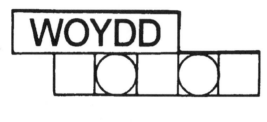

WOYDD

KROJE

SAYMUL

BYTEAU

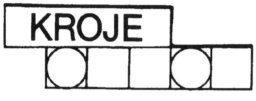

SHE HAD A STEADY JOB TRYING TO KEEP HIM AT THIS.

Now arrange the circled letters to form the surprise answer, as suggested by the above cartoon.

Print answer here A

PUZZLE 41

JUMBLE®

Unscramble these four Jumbles, one letter to each square, to form four ordinary words.

VUSEA

DAIBE

TINEKT

ROBAHR

Guess you've been seeing HER again
A GOLD DIGGER IS ONE WHO HAS WHAT IT TAKES TO DO THIS.

Now arrange the circled letters to form the surprise answer, as suggested by the above cartoon.

Print answer here ☐☐☐☐ WHAT ☐☐☐☐ ☐☐☐☐

PUZZLE 42

JUMBLE®

Unscramble these four Jumbles, one letter to each square, to form four ordinary words.

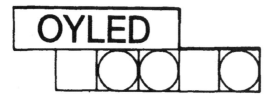

OYLED

GYROP

LINKUE

JOBTEC

This looks like a sure thing
Too risky for me

COULD BE A SKEPTIC'S OUTLOOK.

Now arrange the circled letters to form the surprise answer, as suggested by the above cartoon.

Print answer here A " "

JUMBLE®

Unscramble these four Jumbles, one letter to each square, to form four ordinary words.

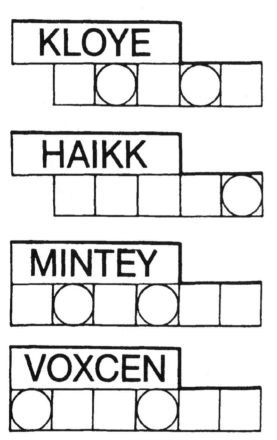

KLOYE

HAIKK

MINTEY

VOXCEN

THE ONLY VOICE THAT DAD SOMETIMES HAS IN FAMILY AFFAIRS.

Now arrange the circled letters to form the surprise answer, as suggested by the above cartoon.

Print answer here " "

PUZZLE 44

JUMBLE®

Unscramble these four Jumbles, one letter to each square, to form four ordinary words.

SURBT

MILTI

CASMIO

FEETOF

WHAT DRACULA GOT WHEN HE MISTOOK A SNOWMAN FOR A HUMAN BEING.

Now arrange the circled letters to form the surprise answer, as suggested by the above cartoon.

Print answer here

PUZZLE 45

JUMBLE®

Unscramble these four Jumbles, one letter to each square, to form four ordinary words.

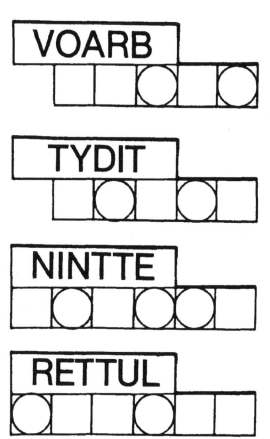

VOARB

TYDIT

NINTTE

RETTUL

WHAT TO PAY IF YOU DON'T WANT TO SPEND TOO MUCH.

Now arrange the circled letters to form the surprise answer, as suggested by the above cartoon.

Print answer here

JUMBLE®

Unscramble these four Jumbles, one letter to each square, to form four ordinary words.

FYMIL

TEQUS

URRUMM

SHUBLE

HE DESERVES TO DO THIS WHEN HE BEHAVES LIKE A WORM.

Now arrange the circled letters to form the surprise answer, as suggested by the above cartoon.

Print answer here

JUMBLE®

Unscramble these four Jumbles, one letter to each square, to form four ordinary words.

NAHEN

JOGIN

DINCIT

INLOPP

FOR HIM, NOTHING WAS SO DIFFICULT AS DOING THIS.

Now arrange the circled letters to form the surprise answer, as suggested by the above cartoon.

Print answer here

PUZZLE 48

JUMBLE®

Unscramble these four Jumbles, one letter to each square, to form four ordinary words.

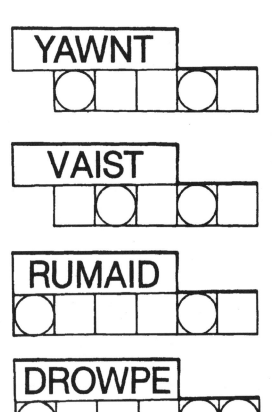

YAWNT

VAIST

RUMAID

DROWPE

THE BEST WAY TO MAKE A LONG STORY SHORT.

Now arrange the circled letters to form the surprise answer, as suggested by the above cartoon.

Print answer here

JUMBLE®

Unscramble these four Jumbles, one letter to each square, to form four ordinary words.

TUFOL

GRAWE

PANUCK

LOACCI

I know my rights!
IGNORANCE OF THE LAW IS NO EXCUSE, ESPECIALLY IF YOU'RE THIS.

Now arrange the circled letters to form the surprise answer, as suggested by the above cartoon.

Print answer here A ____-__-___

PUZZLE 50

JUMBLE®

Unscramble these four Jumbles, one letter to each square, to form four ordinary words.

PORDO

THECK

UCCSAU

CEETIN

SOME PEOPLE THINK THAT A KID WITH TOO MUCH SPUNK MIGHT BENEFIT FROM A LITTLE OF THIS.

Now arrange the circled letters to form the surprise answer, as suggested by the above cartoon.

Print answer here

JUMBLE®

Unscramble these four Jumbles, one letter to each square, to form four ordinary words.

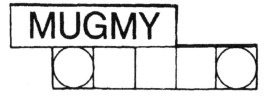

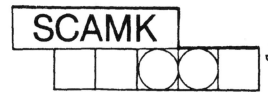

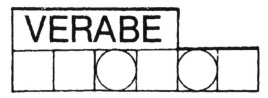

MUGMY

SCAMK

VERABE

RALCOR

What he's got is the best gimmick of all
DAD

THE BEST LABOR-SAVING DEVICE.

Now arrange the circled letters to form the surprise answer, as suggested by the above cartoon.

Print answer here

JUMBLE®

Unscramble these four Jumbles, one letter to each square, to form four ordinary words.

VAROS

MURYM

TISSAD

YAIRFT

He's doing the right thing
SOME SAY THAT IF YOU MARRY A WIDOW YOU WON'T DO THIS.

Now arrange the circled letters to form the surprise answer, as suggested by the above cartoon.

Print answer here ☐☐☐☐☐ "☐-☐☐☐☐"

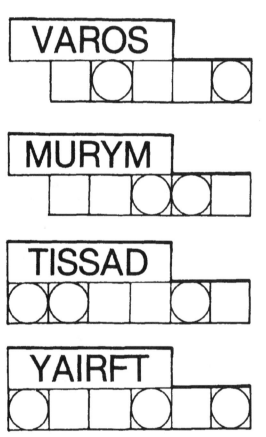

PUZZLE 53

JUMBLE®

Unscramble these four Jumbles, one letter to each square, to form four ordinary words.

CRAFS

LIPUP

ENJUKT

BUSUDE

WHAT THE TEACHER DID WHEN THE ANTELOPE TOOK HIS FINAL EXAM.

Now arrange the circled letters to form the surprise answer, as suggested by the above cartoon.

Print answer here ○○○○○○ THE ○○○○

PUZZLE
54

JUMBLE®

Unscramble these four Jumbles, one letter to each square, to form four ordinary words.

YEMON

RUPOC

CRUVSY

TREMIC

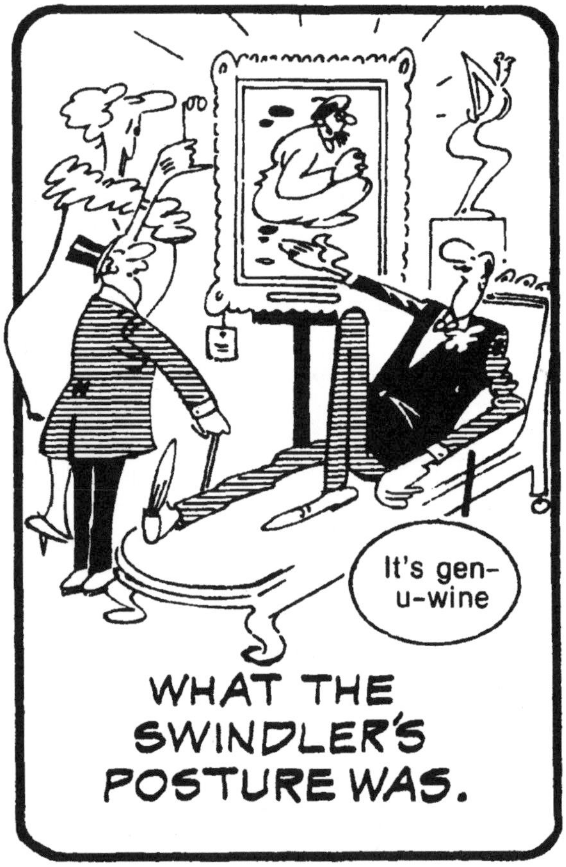
It's gen-
u-wine
WHAT THE
SWINDLER'S
POSTURE WAS.

Now arrange the circled letters to form the surprise answer, as suggested by the above cartoon.

Print answer here " "

PUZZLE 55

JUMBLE®

Unscramble these four Jumbles, one letter to each square, to form four ordinary words.

ELVOH

MOIFT

DANAGE

RILIXE

I move for a mistrial
A JURY NEVER WORKS RIGHT WHEN IT'S THIS.

Now arrange the circled letters to form the surprise answer, as suggested by the above cartoon.

Print answer here " "

PUZZLE 56

JUMBLE®

Unscramble these four Jumbles, one letter to each square, to form four ordinary words.

PHARY

ISTUE

SEIBED

CORTER

We've all gone out. Your food is in the refrigerator
WHAT SOME PEOPLE'S HAND-WRITING IS.

Now arrange the circled letters to form the surprise answer, as suggested by the above cartoon.

Print answer here A " "

PUZZLE 57

JUMBLE®

Unscramble these four Jumbles, one letter to each square, to form four ordinary words.

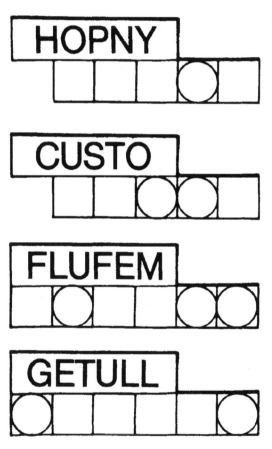

HOPNY

CUSTO

FLUFEM

GETULL

WHERE'S THE FENCING MASTER?

Now arrange the circled letters to form the surprise answer, as suggested by the above cartoon.

Print answer here ☐☐☐ TO "☐☐☐☐☐☐"

PUZZLE 58

JUMBLE®

Unscramble these four Jumbles, one letter to each square, to form four ordinary words.

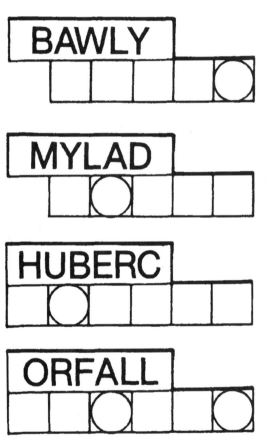

BAWLY

MYLAD

HUBERC

ORFALL

WHAT THEY THOUGHT IT WAS WHEN THE WIMP TRIED TO ACT LIKE A WOLF.

Now arrange the circled letters to form the surprise answer, as suggested by the above cartoon.

Print answer here ☐ "☐☐☐☐☐"

JUMBLE®

Unscramble these four Jumbles, one letter to each square, to form four ordinary words.

HINEW

PHLYS

SLYJUT

RARQUY

It's amazing how he comes up with them on the spur of the moment
WHAT THE STAND-UP COMEDIAN EQUIPS HIMSELF WITH.

Now arrange the circled letters to form the surprise answer, as suggested by the above cartoon.

Print answer here

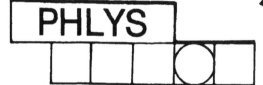

PUZZLE 60

JUMBLE®

Unscramble these four Jumbles, one letter to each square, to form four ordinary words.

YESTT

JAHAR

HOWALL

PYSEDE

They really take their workouts seriously
COULD THIS BE ANOTHER NAME FOR THAT HEALTH CLUB?

Now arrange the circled letters to form the surprise answer, as suggested by the above cartoon.

Print answer here THE " "

JUMBLE®

Unscramble these four Jumbles, one letter to each square, to form four ordinary words.

YOIRN

USCOT

WYLLOH

NOBENT

Listen to how I play this
He thinks he's the best
WHAT THE SELF-CENTERED TRUMPET PLAYER LIKED TO DO.

Now arrange the circled letters to form the surprise answer, as suggested by the above cartoon.

Print answer here ◯◯◯◯ HIS ◯◯◯ ◯◯◯◯

PUZZLE 62

JUMBLE®

Unscramble these four Jumbles, one letter to each square, to form four ordinary words.

DUGAR

PRAVO

SUREDS

DEECES

WHERE THE WOMEN OFFICERS ENJOYED GOING WHILE OFF DUTY.

Now arrange the circled letters to form the surprise answer, as suggested by the above cartoon.

Print answer here TO A

JUMBLE®

Unscramble these four Jumbles, one letter to each square, to form four ordinary words.

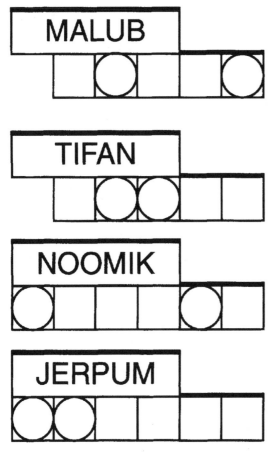

MALUB

TIFAN

NOOMIK

JERPUM

WHAT THE POST-
MAN DELIVERED
TO THE CHINESE
VESSEL.

Now arrange the circled letters to form the surprise answer, as suggested by the above cartoon.

Print answer here

PUZZLE 64

JUMBLE®

Unscramble these four Jumbles, one letter to each square, to form four ordinary words.

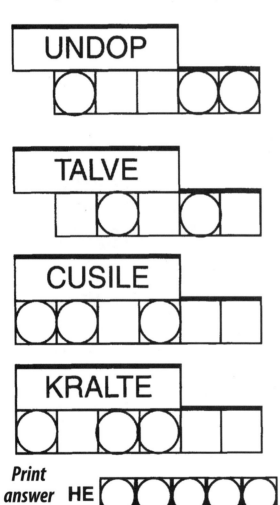

UNDOP

TALVE

CUSILE

KRALTE

What are you going to do with them?
SOLD
SOLD
They're good investments
WHY THE BOTA-NIST BOUGHT THE FACTORIES.

Now arrange the circled letters to form the surprise answer, as suggested by the above cartoon.

Print answer here HE "   "

PUZZLE 65

JUMBLE®

Unscramble these four Jumbles, one letter to each square, to form four ordinary words.

TIFFY

NAGET

NIMERV

FAINAR

... and if I'm elected, I'll ...
Same old campaign promises

WHAT THE CROOKED POLITICIAN WANTED THE WHISTLE-STOP TOUR TO TURN INTO.

Now arrange the circled letters to form the surprise answer, as suggested by the above cartoon.

Print answer here **THE**

JUMBLE®

Unscramble these four Jumbles, one letter to each square, to form four ordinary words.

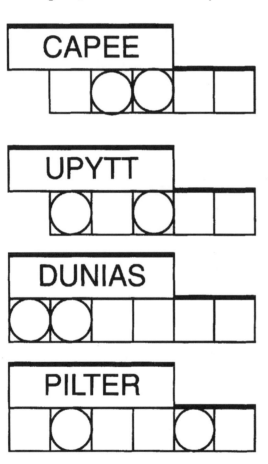

CAPEE

UPYTT

DUNIAS

PILTER

Excuse us!
That's awful
AN OFF-COLOR JOKE MADE THEM DO THIS.

Now arrange the circled letters to form the surprise answer, as suggested by the above cartoon.

Print answer here

JUMBLE®

Unscramble these four Jumbles, one letter to each square, to form four ordinary words.

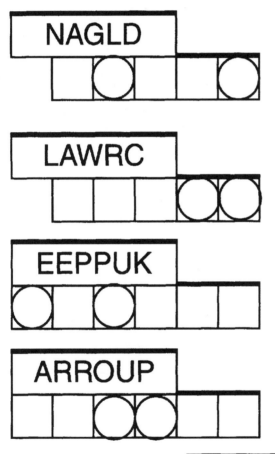

NAGLD

LAWRC

EEPPUK

ARROUP

Isn't it boring?
I meet lots of people
WHAT THE KNIFE SHARPENER CONSIDERED HIS JOB.

Now arrange the circled letters to form the surprise answer, as suggested by the above cartoon.

Print answer here " ◯◯◯◯ " ◯◯◯◯

JUMBLE®

Unscramble these four Jumbles, one letter to each square, to form four ordinary words.

LAWRD

UNERP

LIDIAN

ELLAHT

Lots of valuables in this bag
A GOOD THING TO HOLD ONTO WHEN TAKING A FLIGHT.

Now arrange the circled letters to form the surprise answer, as suggested by the above cartoon.

Print answer here **THE**

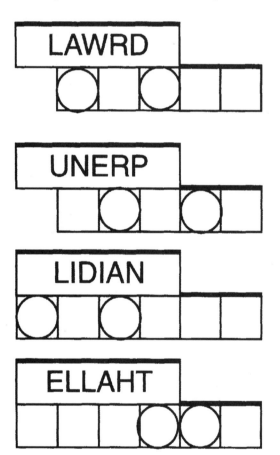

JUMBLE®

Unscramble these four Jumbles, one letter to each square, to form four ordinary words.

WYSOH

NAHEN

INCOVE

MACENE

TOO MANY OF THESE CAN MAKE YOU SICK ON A CRUISE.

Now arrange the circled letters to form the surprise answer, as suggested by the above cartoon.

Print answer here

PUZZLE 70

JUMBLE®

Unscramble these four Jumbles, one letter to each square, to form four ordinary words.

Perfect
HOW THE STU-
DENT MANICURIST
DID ON HER EXAM.

ARRIB

PAADT

MELING

FLANEL

Now arrange the circled letters to form the surprise answer, as suggested by the above cartoon.

Print answer here **SHE** " "

PUZZLE 71

JUMBLE®

Unscramble these four Jumbles, one letter to each square, to form four ordinary words.

SABSI

TABEA

ALVASS

TRYPAN

He watches everything
ALWAYS KEPT BY A RESTAURANT OWNER.

Now arrange the circled letters to form the surprise answer, as suggested by the above cartoon.

Print answer here ON THE

JUMBLE®

Unscramble these four Jumbles, one letter to each square, to form four ordinary words.

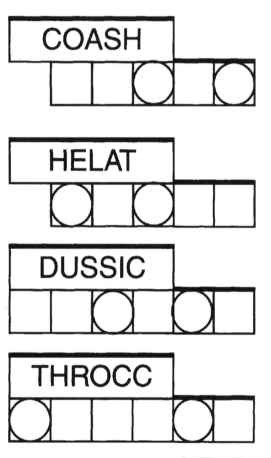

COASH

HELAT

DUSSIC

THROCC

Remember, just a little at a time

GOOD STUDENTS AT A BARBER COLLEGE WILL DO THIS.

Now arrange the circled letters to form the surprise answer, as suggested by the above cartoon.

Print answer here ___ A _____

PUZZLE 73

JUMBLE®

Unscramble these four Jumbles, one letter to each square, to form four ordinary words.

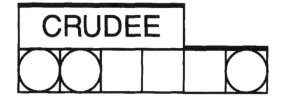

GRITE

TUISE

VINNET

CRUDEE

Now arrange the circled letters to form the surprise answer, as suggested by the above cartoon.

Print answer here “ - ”

PUZZLE 74

JUMBLE®

Unscramble these four Jumbles, one letter to each square, to form four ordinary words.

OCCIL

TOCET

RELENK

VOUDER

Simply breathtaking
Hey how about our picture?
THIS HAPPENED TO HIS WORK AT THE SCENIC CANYON.

Now arrange the circled letters to form the surprise answer, as suggested by the above cartoon.

Print answer here HE " ____________ " IT

PUZZLE 75

JUMBLE®

Unscramble these four Jumbles, one letter to each square, to form four ordinary words.

JICUE

PRUCO

CHETOL

KHENAS

THE FIRST THING THE EX-BOXER WAS ASKED TO DO IN HIS NEW JOB.

Now arrange the circled letters to form the surprise answer, as suggested by the above cartoon.

Print answer here THE

PUZZLE 76

JUMBLE®

Unscramble these four Jumbles, one letter to each square, to form four ordinary words.

GADMO

THRAW

LOUTAW

LUFUES

Time to get up
#$%*!!
THE SLEEPY FARMER RESPONDED TO THE ROOSTER WITH THIS.

Now arrange the circled letters to form the surprise answer, as suggested by the above cartoon.

Print answer here " "

PUZZLE 77

JUMBLE®

Unscramble these four Jumbles, one letter to each square, to form four ordinary words.

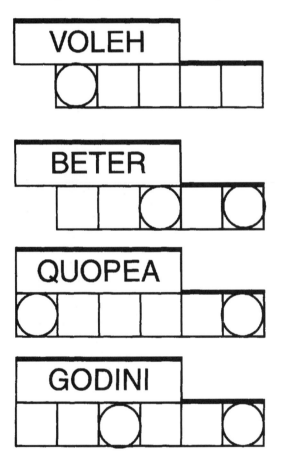

VOLEH

BETER

QUOPEA

GODINI

How about a kiss?
How 'bout you leave?

WHAT SHE SHOWED HER OBNOXIOUS DATE.

Now arrange the circled letters to form the surprise answer, as suggested by the above cartoon.

Print answer here

JUMBLE®

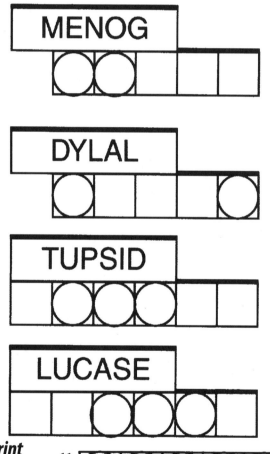

Unscramble these four Jumbles, one letter to each square, to form four ordinary words.

MENOG

DYLAL

TUPSID

LUCASE

WHAT KIND OF HUMORIST WAS THE COMIC?

Now arrange the circled letters to form the surprise answer, as suggested by the above cartoon.

Print answer here **A** " - "

JUMBLE®

Unscramble these four Jumbles, one letter to each square, to form four ordinary words.

NIMEC

TABLO

WRALEY

YULNOH

Your taxes worked out perfectly
THE TIGHTROPE WALKER HIRED THE ACCOUNTANT BECAUSE HE KNEW ---

Now arrange the circled letters to form the surprise answer, as suggested by the above cartoon.

Print answer here ___ TO _______

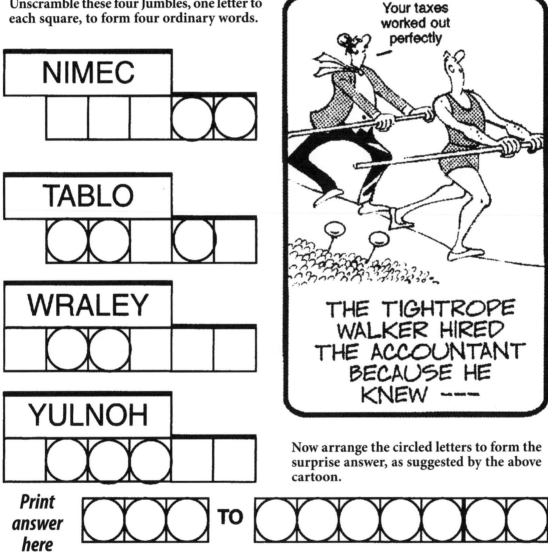

JUMBLE®

Unscramble these four Jumbles, one letter to each square, to form four ordinary words.

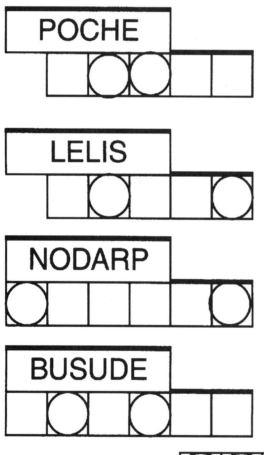

POCHE

LELIS

NODARP

BUSUDE

WHAT THE POLO PLAYER DID WHEN THE BILL CAME FOR THE DRINKS.

Now arrange the circled letters to form the surprise answer, as suggested by the above cartoon.

Print answer here " "

JUMBLE®

Unscramble these four Jumbles, one letter to each square, to form four ordinary words.

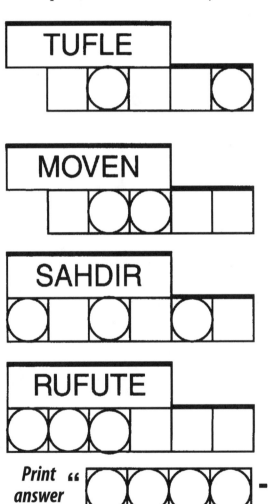

TUFLE

MOVEN

SAHDIR

RUFUTE

WHAT FIDO ENJOYED AS THE FAMILY FINISHED DINNER.

Now arrange the circled letters to form the surprise answer, as suggested by the above cartoon.

Print answer here " - "

JUMBLE®

Unscramble these four Jumbles, one letter to each square, to form four ordinary words.

KULCC

DYRIT

DORMEN

WOCALL

This is a rough job
Yeah, but we'll be rich
DRILLING FOR OIL IS ALWAYS THIS.

Now arrange the circled letters to form the surprise answer, as suggested by the above cartoon.

Print answer here " "

PUZZLE 83

JUMBLE®

Unscramble these four Jumbles, one letter to each square, to form four ordinary words.

GOROF

KAQUE

GINBUL

DREHWS

Look, how quaint
WHAT THE DENTIST ADMIRED ON HIS ROAD TRIP.

Now arrange the circled letters to form the surprise answer, as suggested by the above cartoon.

Print answer here **THE**

JUMBLE®

Unscramble these four Jumbles, one letter to each square, to form four ordinary words.

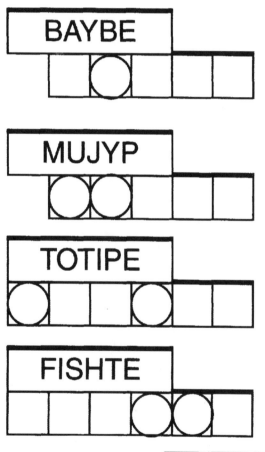

BAYBE

MUJYP

TOTIPE

FISHTE

This work takes patience and skill

DOES IT TAKE A LOT TO USE A BRACE?

Now arrange the circled letters to form the surprise answer, as suggested by the above cartoon.

Print answer here A “ ”

PUZZLE 85

JUMBLE®

Unscramble these four Jumbles, one letter to each square, to form four ordinary words.

HERBT

SOUMY

KOTLEC

TREEWP

You did a good job today
He's here 16 hours a day
WHAT IT TAKES TO TRAIN A THOROUGHBRED.

Now arrange the circled letters to form the surprise answer, as suggested by the above cartoon.

Print answer here **A**

JUMBLE®

Unscramble these four Jumbles, one letter to each square, to form four ordinary words.

YONPE

UNEES

OETAGE

CLAJAK

Where are the strawberries?
He'll disappear when the check arrives
THE FREELOADER'S FAVORITE DESSERT.

Now arrange the circled letters to form the surprise answer, as suggested by the above cartoon.

Print answer here " "

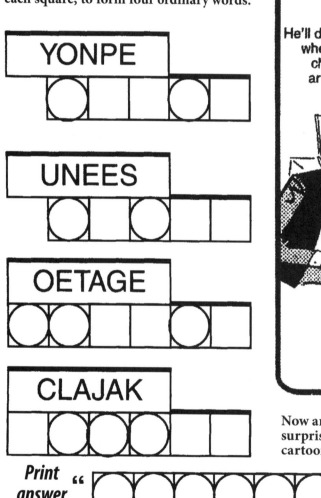

PUZZLE 87

JUMBLE®

Unscramble these four Jumbles, one letter to each square, to form four ordinary words.

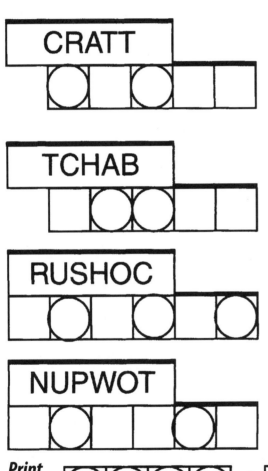

CRATT

TCHAB

RUSHOC

NUPWOT

WHAT THE DESIGNER SAID WHEN THE GAR-MENT WAS DONE.

Now arrange the circled letters to form the surprise answer, as suggested by the above cartoon.

Print answer here ____ ' _ A " _____ "

JUMBLE®

Unscramble these four Jumbles, one letter to each square, to form four ordinary words.

TILUQ

STEAE

RUQRAY

FONLEY

SURE TO BE THIS AFTER A NIGHT ON THE TOWN.

Now arrange the circled letters to form the surprise answer, as suggested by the above cartoon.

Print answer here

PUZZLE 89

JUMBLE®

Unscramble these four Jumbles, one letter to each square, to form four ordinary words.

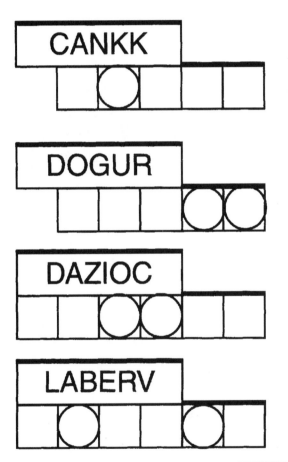

CANKK

DOGUR

DAZIOC

LABERV

Good as new
FIXING THE KITCHEN SINK LEFT POP LIKE THIS.

Now arrange the circled letters to form the surprise answer, as suggested by the above cartoon.

Print answer here " "

PUZZLE 90

JUMBLE®

Unscramble these four Jumbles, one letter to each square, to form four ordinary words.

TYJET

NENLI

TOOLEC

LANDOU

I'm prompt and dependable
THE CENSUS TAKER WAS HIRED BECAUSE HE COULD ---

Now arrange the circled letters to form the surprise answer, as suggested by the above cartoon.

Print answer here BE " "

JUMBLE®

Unscramble these four Jumbles, one letter to each square, to form four ordinary words.

CLEEX

LYKIM

GERDED

LASSIA

You're a picture of sartorial splendor
WHEN HE ARRIVED FOR THE HUNT HE WAS ---

Now arrange the circled letters to form the surprise answer, as suggested by the above cartoon.

Print answer here TO " "

JUMBLE®

Unscramble these four Jumbles, one letter to
each square, to form four ordinary words.

HIWSS

PRIGE

SLAVIE

NIFTIE

I eat every other day

WHAT A CRASH
DIET CAN LEAD
TO.

Now arrange the circled letters to form the
surprise answer, as suggested by the above
cartoon.

Print
answer
here " ◯◯◯◯ "   ◯◯◯◯◯◯

JUMBLE®

Unscramble these four Jumbles, one letter to each square, to form four ordinary words.

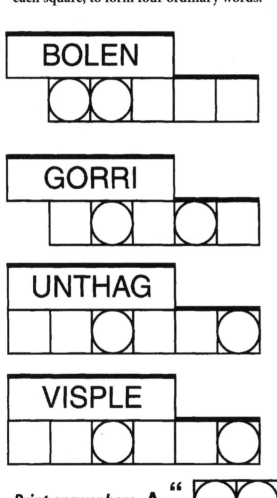

BOLEN

GORRI

UNTHAG

VISPLE

Now arrange the circled letters to form the surprise answer, as suggested by the above cartoon.

Print answer here A " "

JUMBLE®

Unscramble these four Jumbles, one letter to each square, to form four ordinary words.

GALEE

GAMLE

ALOONG

SHARTH

Here's your order, pilgrim
He thinks he's John Wayne
SERVED BY THE ASPIRING ACTOR AT THE BREAK-FAST COUNTER.

Now arrange the circled letters to form the surprise answer, as suggested by the above cartoon.

Print answer here " " AND

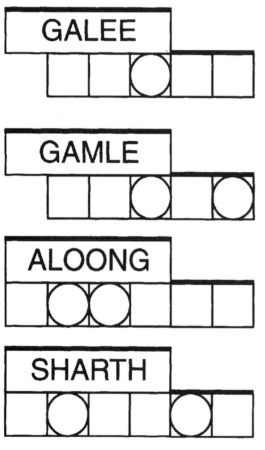

PUZZLE

95

JUMBLE®

Unscramble these four Jumbles, one letter to each square, to form four ordinary words.

RITHM

SYTUM

SMUQIR

KLUNIE

Now arrange the circled letters to form the surprise answer, as suggested by the above cartoon.

Print answer here ○○○○○ A ○○○○

PUZZLE 96

JUMBLE®

Unscramble these four Jumbles, one letter to each square, to form four ordinary words.

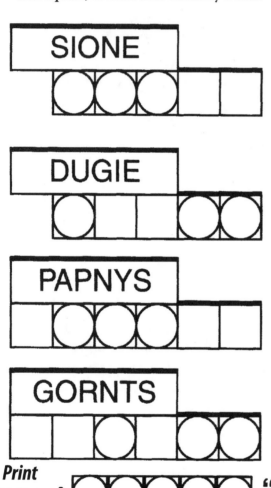

SIONE

DUGIE

PAPNYS

GORNTS

Welcome
On the house
PFSSST

WHAT THE CUSTOMER EXPERIENCED WHEN HE VISITED THE NEW PUB.

Now arrange the circled letters to form the surprise answer, as suggested by the above cartoon.

Print answer here A "   "

JUMBLE®

Unscramble these four Jumbles, one letter to each square, to form four ordinary words.

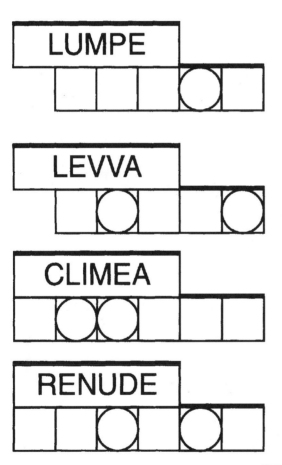

LUMPE

LEVVA

CLIMEA

RENUDE

What's wrong -- You OK?
Going fishing
WHEN HE WAS AWAKENED EARLY, HIS WIFE WAS ---

Now arrange the circled letters to form the surprise answer, as suggested by the above cartoon.

Print answer here

PUZZLE 98

JUMBLE®

Unscramble these four Jumbles, one letter to each square, to form four ordinary words.

SLARN

SEPIO

THOTEG

LARNAC

Don't forget my spikes
WHAT THE KIDS TURNED DAD'S VAN INTO.

Now arrange the circled letters to form the surprise answer, as suggested by the above cartoon.

Print answer here **A** " ______ " ____

PUZZLE 99

JUMBLE®

Unscramble these four Jumbles, one letter to each square, to form four ordinary words.

BLAWR

WULFA

EMBURP

CEDITE

She's very protective
They're beautiful
HOW THE LIONESS FELT WHEN SUR-ROUNDED BY HER CUBS.

Now arrange the circled letters to form the surprise answer, as suggested by the above cartoon.

Print answer here OF “ ”

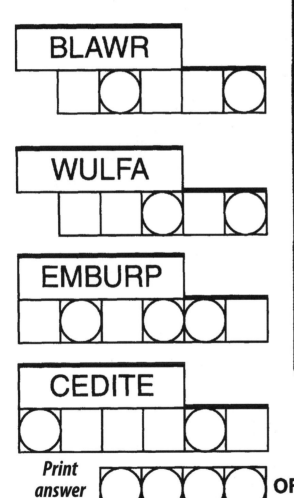

JUMBLE®

Unscramble these four Jumbles, one letter to each square, to form four ordinary words.

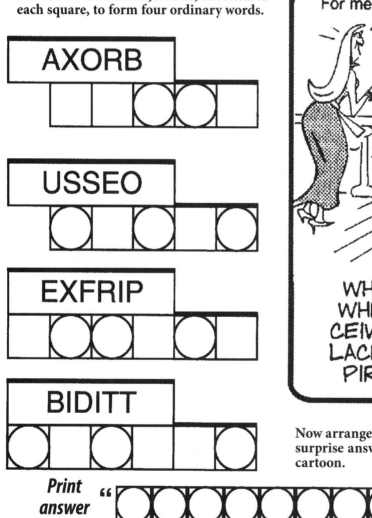

AXORB

USSEO

EXFRIP

BIDITT

For me? I'll always wear it

WHAT SHE DID WHEN SHE RE-CEIVED A NECK-LACE FROM THE PIRATE CHEST.

Now arrange the circled letters to form the surprise answer, as suggested by the above cartoon.

Print answer here " ◯◯◯◯◯◯◯◯◯ " ◯◯

JUMBLE®

Unscramble these four Jumbles, one letter to each square, to form four ordinary words.

FYNAC

LOHLE

RAYSOV

MABGIT

It's so noisy in here
Everyone's gabbing

WHAT THE COMPUTER STAFF CONSIDERED THE BREAK LOUNGE.

Now arrange the circled letters to form the surprise answer, as suggested by the above cartoon.

Print answer here **A**

JUMBLE®

Unscramble these four Jumbles, one letter to each square, to form four ordinary words.

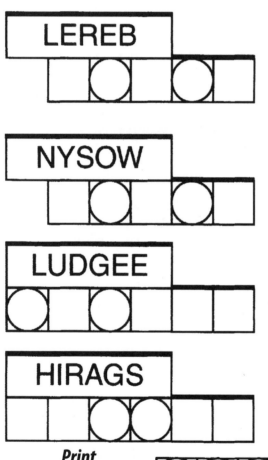

LEREB

NYSOW

LUDGEE

HIRAGS

WHEN THE STUDENTS GOT UNRULY, THE ART TEACHER DID THIS.

Now arrange the circled letters to form the surprise answer, as suggested by the above cartoon.

Print answer here **HE** ( ) ( ) ( ) ( ) **THE** ( ) ( ) ( ) ( )

PUZZLE 103

JUMBLE®

Unscramble these four Jumbles, one letter to each square, to form four ordinary words.

SETTY

RAPPE

YIRCKT

ENTINY

Uh, oh -- she's not laughing
WHAT SHE GAVE HIM AFTER HER SPILL AT THE SKATING RINK.

Now arrange the circled letters to form the surprise answer, as suggested by the above cartoon.

Print answer here **AN** " ◯◯◯ " ◯◯◯◯◯

PUZZLE 104

JUMBLE®

Unscramble these four Jumbles, one letter to each square, to form four ordinary words.

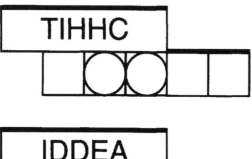

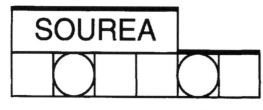

TIHHC

IDDEA

TEETIP

SOUREA

The Giants will run over them
No way
Barkeep, another one

A CONVERSATION AT A SPORTS BAR CAN BECOME THIS.

Now arrange the circled letters to form the surprise answer, as suggested by the above cartoon.

Print answer here " "

PUZZLE 105

JUMBLE®

Unscramble these four Jumbles, one letter to each square, to form four ordinary words.

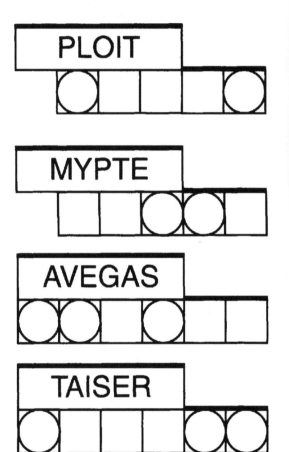

PLOIT

MYPTE

AVEGAS

TAISER

You're late. No dinner tonight
WHY JUNIOR DIDN'T GET ANY SUPPER.

Now arrange the circled letters to form the surprise answer, as suggested by the above cartoon.

Print answer here IT WAS

JUMBLE®

Unscramble these four Jumbles, one letter to each square, to form four ordinary words.

OSOME

MALLA

LUPPIT

ETEELY

By the way, I need a parking permit
WHAT THE DENTIST AND THE MAYOR SHARED.

Now arrange the circled letters to form the surprise answer, as suggested by the above cartoon.

Print answer here OF " "

PUZZLE 107

JUMBLE®

Unscramble these four Jumbles, one letter to each square, to form four ordinary words.

DICHE

FLAIN

WEVILS

NAUTER

The salesman could be a model
TO BE SUCCESS-FUL, A CLOTHING RETAILER MUST ALWAYS BE---

Now arrange the circled letters to form the surprise answer, as suggested by the above cartoon.

Print answer here ◯◯◯◯ - ◯◯◯◯◯◯

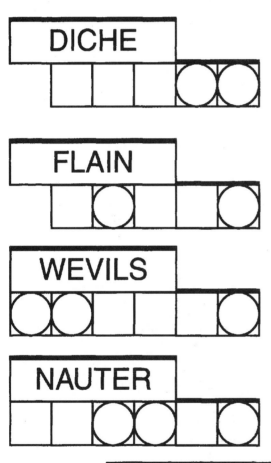

PUZZLE 108

JUMBLE®

Unscramble these four Jumbles, one letter to each square, to form four ordinary words.

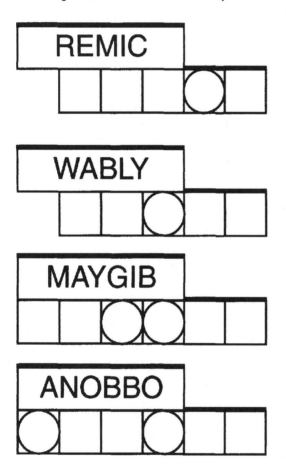

REMIC

WABLY

MAYGIB

ANOBBO

I knew I'd make it
SCREECH!

WHAT HE TOOK WHEN HE RAN ACROSS THE STREET.

Now arrange the circled letters to form the surprise answer, as suggested by the above cartoon.

Print answer here A " "

JUMBLE®

Unscramble these four Jumbles, one letter to each square, to form four ordinary words.

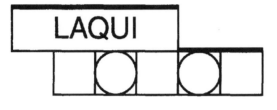

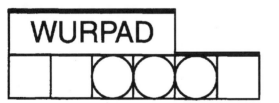

LAQUI

HALCK

NURPEY

WURPAD

This game wins the championship
I'll break

WHAT THE POOL PLAYER WANTED TO DO.

Now arrange the circled letters to form the surprise answer, as suggested by the above cartoon.

Print answer here ____ __ A ___

PUZZLE 110

JUMBLE®

Unscramble these four Jumbles, one letter to each square, to form four ordinary words.

STOIF

RUFOL

YORRAM

GURTED

You live in this mess?
What's wrong?

NOBODY IS SURPRISED WHEN "DORMITORY" IS TURNED INTO THIS.

Now arrange the circled letters to form the surprise answer, as suggested by the above cartoon.

Print answer here

PUZZLE 111

JUMBLE®

Unscramble these four Jumbles, one letter to each square, to form four ordinary words.

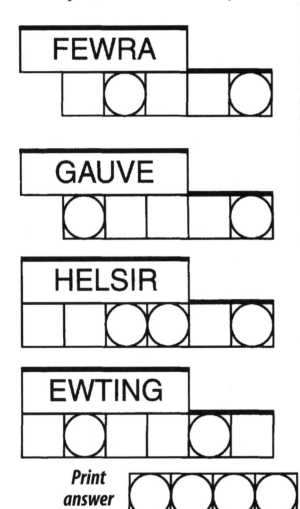

FEWRA

GAUVE

HELSIR

EWTING

WHAT HE DID WHEN THE CEILING FAN NEEDED REPAIR.

Now arrange the circled letters to form the surprise answer, as suggested by the above cartoon.

Print answer here ◯◯◯◯ IT A ◯◯◯◯◯

JUMBLE®

Unscramble these four Jumbles, one letter to each square, to form four ordinary words.

BAZLE

OVERP

DROWPE

LEBALT

Hurry up! I'll be late for lunch
I'll be done in a minute.
WHAT THE HAIR-DRESSER DID WHEN THE CUSTOMER GOT NASTY.

Now arrange the circled letters to form the surprise answer, as suggested by the above cartoon.

Print answer here ( ) ( ) ( ) ( ) HER ( ) ( ) ( )

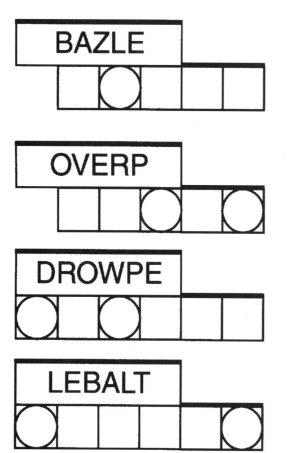

PUZZLE 113

JUMBLE®

Unscramble these four Jumbles, one letter to each square, to form four ordinary words.

RUILD

ACTUD

BANCOR

ELDAHN

Where're his manners?
He didn't even kiss your hand
THIS RESULTED WHEN THE FRENCH-MAN DIDN'T SAY GOOD-BYE.

Now arrange the circled letters to form the surprise answer, as suggested by the above cartoon.

Print answer here ◯◯◯ **OVER** ◯◯◯◯◯

JUMBLE®

Unscramble these four Jumbles, one letter to each square, to form four ordinary words.

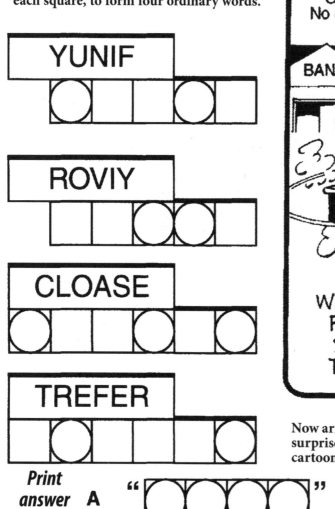

YUNIF

ROVIY

CLOASE

TREFER

Go thataway...
No one will see us
BANK

WHAT THE CARE-FUL ROBBERS SOUGHT FOR THEIR GETAWAY.

Now arrange the circled letters to form the surprise answer, as suggested by the above cartoon.

Print answer here **A** “◯◯◯◯” ◯◯◯◯◯

JUMBLE®

Unscramble these four Jumbles, one letter to each square, to form four ordinary words.

FECAH

GENUB

DRUSAB

SLAQUL

...and did you hear the one about...
He's awful
What's so funny about that?
THE COMEDY CON- TESTANT WAS SO BAD, THEY SAID HIS ROUTINE WAS —

Now arrange the circled letters to form the surprise answer, as suggested by the above cartoon.

Print answer here " "

PUZZLE 116

JUMBLE®

Unscramble these four Jumbles, one letter to each square, to form four ordinary words.

DOLYD

BUTIC

RATHEH

STEWID

WHAT THE COOK DID WHEN THE SERVER DROPPED THE TRAY.

Now arrange the circled letters to form the surprise answer, as suggested by the above cartoon.

Print answer here " " IT

JUMBLE®

Unscramble these four Jumbles, one letter to each square, to form four ordinary words.

CHOLT

RABIN

NAUVEE

AGGIZZ

TOO MUCH BEER CAN LEAD TO THIS.

Now arrange the circled letters to form the surprise answer, as suggested by the above cartoon.

Print answer here **A** " "

PUZZLE 118

JUMBLE®

Unscramble these four Jumbles, one letter to each square, to form four ordinary words.

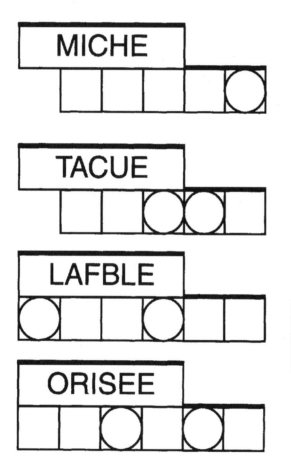

MICHE

TACUE

LAFBLE

ORISEE

WHAT SHE GAVE HER BOYFRIEND FOR HIS BIRTHDAY.

Now arrange the circled letters to form the surprise answer, as suggested by the above cartoon.

Print answer here **A** “   ”

JUMBLE®

Unscramble these four Jumbles, one letter to each square, to form four ordinary words.

SAREE

SLUPH

COATEL

SNIFUE

I can't wait for this every year
FOR MANY, SKIING TURNS WINTER INTO THIS.

Now arrange the circled letters to form the surprise answer, as suggested by the above cartoon.

Print answer here THE "◯◯◯◯" ◯◯◯◯◯◯

JUMBLE®

Unscramble these four Jumbles, one letter to each square, to form four ordinary words.

SPEHE

LOVEN

TYRITH

PONISH

Sell ten thousand
OFTEN EXER-
CISED BY A
SUCCESSFUL
EXECUTIVE.

Now arrange the circled letters to form the surprise answer, as suggested by the above cartoon.

Print answer here

JUMBLE®

Unscramble these four Jumbles, one letter to each square, to form four ordinary words.

NOBAT

CNATH

SIMREY

TESSMY

SCREECH!
Not bad
WHAT SHE TOOK TO APPEAR IN THE HORROR MOVIE.

Now arrange the circled letters to form the surprise answer, as suggested by the above cartoon.

Print answer here A " "

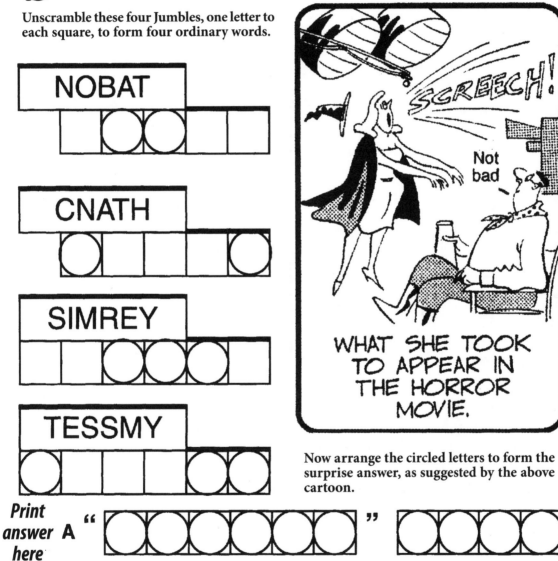

PUZZLE 122

JUMBLE®

Unscramble these four Jumbles, one letter to each square, to form four ordinary words.

SERCS

VONEY

WHEENP

WALLOF

With your prices, you must be rich
A TAILOR'S BUSINESS IS USUALLY THIS.

Now arrange the circled letters to form the surprise answer, as suggested by the above cartoon.

Print answer here

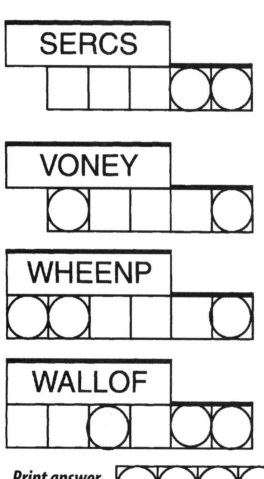

JUMBLE®

Unscramble these four Jumbles, one letter to each square, to form four ordinary words.

DUHMI

TEVEN

RYBBAC

CAULNY

Keep your head down, and swing through
HOW HE DROVE DOWN THE FAIRWAY.

Now arrange the circled letters to form the surprise answer, as suggested by the above cartoon.

Print answer here ◯◯ A ◯◯◯◯

PUZZLE 124

JUMBLE®

Unscramble these four Jumbles, one letter to each square, to form four ordinary words.

PLUIP

VELOC

LOWALT

YENICT

Her feminine charms worked
They dated forever
WHAT IT TOOK TO GET HIM TO THE ALTAR.

Now arrange the circled letters to form the surprise answer, as suggested by the above cartoon.

Print answer here **A** ______ "____"

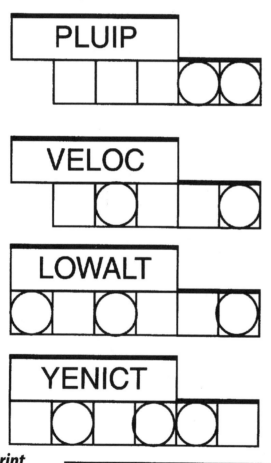

PUZZLE 125

JUMBLE®

Unscramble these four Jumbles, one letter to each square, to form four ordinary words.

GWEED

JOMAR

LENZOZ

MOYGOL

Looks like rain
It should help our crops
THE FARMER WANTED TO SEE THIS.

Now arrange the circled letters to form the surprise answer, as suggested by the above cartoon.

Print answer here **HIS**

PUZZLE 126

JUMBLE®

Unscramble these four Jumbles, one letter to each square, to form four ordinary words.

RUCRY

KYASH

COULIN

MUBHEL

I told you to fill up
I thought I could make it
GAS TWO MILES

WHAT HE PUSHED WHEN HE RAN OUT OF GAS.

Now arrange the circled letters to form the surprise answer, as suggested by the above cartoon.

Print answer here

PUZZLE 127

JUMBLE®

Unscramble these four Jumbles, one letter to each square, to form four ordinary words.

VERAB

DINEK

LUNYUR

MAYLIF

This will give us a lift
We need that 15 minute rest
TO A MECHANIC, COFFEE IS OFTEN THIS.

Now arrange the circled letters to form the surprise answer, as suggested by the above cartoon.

Print answer here " "

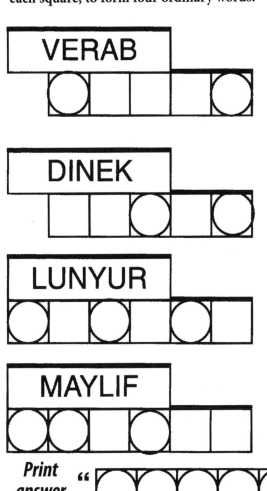

PUZZLE 128

JUMBLE®

Unscramble these four Jumbles, one letter to each square, to form four ordinary words.

SEUDO

LITAP

MYDOBE

MOURUQ

I must say you're not too expensive
WHAT THE REASONABLE FORTUNE-TELLER CHARGED.

Now arrange the circled letters to form the surprise answer, as suggested by the above cartoon.

Print answer here " "

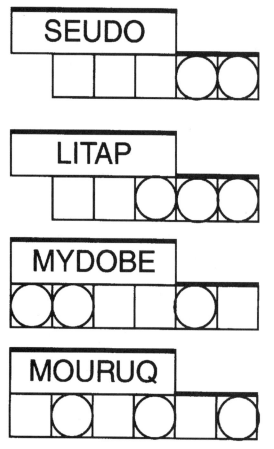

JUMBLE®

Unscramble these four Jumbles, one letter to each square, to form four ordinary words.

FENTO

NORTS

STOLJE

TIPEOA

He's a real eager beaver
LOW RATES
IT TAKES THIS TO BECOME A SUCCESSFUL BANKER.

Now arrange the circled letters to form the surprise answer, as suggested by the above cartoon.

Print answer here ____ OF ________

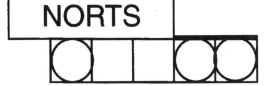

PUZZLE 130

JUMBLE®

Unscramble these four Jumbles, one letter to each square, to form four ordinary words.

CNAEP

KONET

NATTEX

MACPIT

It gets more complicated every year
PREPARING AN ANNUAL RETURN CAN DO THIS.

Now arrange the circled letters to form the surprise answer, as suggested by the above cartoon.

Print answer here

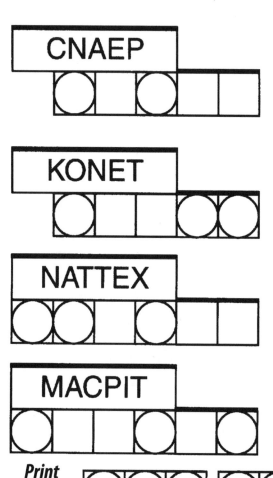

PUZZLE 131

JUMBLE®

Unscramble these four Jumbles, one letter to each square, to form four ordinary words.

NARPO

YELCC

TEASTE

MIENER

Dad, why is that one black?

WHAT ONE OUT OF TEN COWS IS.

Now arrange the circled letters to form the surprise answer, as suggested by the above cartoon.

Print answer here

JUMBLE®

Unscramble these four Jumbles, one letter to each square, to form four ordinary words.

ELCHE

LIXEE

DANUSE

SLOIPH

Wave hello to her majesty
WHERE THE QUEEN WAS OFTEN SEEN.

Now arrange the circled letters to form the surprise answer, as suggested by the above cartoon.

Print answer here ◯◯ "◯◯" ◯◯◯◯◯◯

JUMBLE®

Unscramble these four Jumbles, one letter to each square, to form four ordinary words.

DALLE

HOCKE

LARCIA

STACOM

He's got money to burn
THIS GIVES A MISER A WARM FEELING.

Now arrange the circled letters to form the surprise answer, as suggested by the above cartoon.

Print answer here

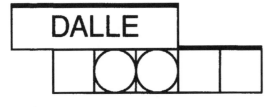

PUZZLE 134

JUMBLE®

Unscramble these four Jumbles, one letter to each square, to form four ordinary words.

SOINY

YUHRR

SHURTH

ANDAGE

Another hour 'til we land
I'm dying of thirst
HOW THE PAS-SENGERS FELT WHEN THEIR LATE FLIGHT RAN OUT OF DRINKS.

Now arrange the circled letters to form the surprise answer, as suggested by the above cartoon.

Print answer here ☐☐☐☐ AND ☐☐☐

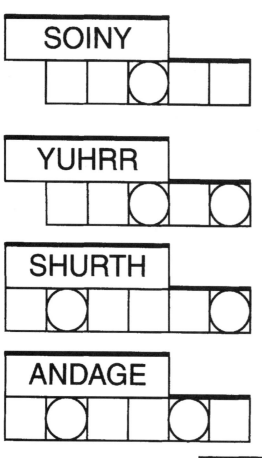

JUMBLE®

Unscramble these four Jumbles, one letter to each square, to form four ordinary words.

GOBEF

MEENY

FALLTY

ROBRAW

Brr -- can't wait to sit by the fire

WHAT THE WEATHERMAN LONGED FOR ON A SUBZERO NIGHT.

Now arrange the circled letters to form the surprise answer, as suggested by the above cartoon.

Print answer here A

PUZZLE 136

JUMBLE®

Unscramble these four Jumbles, one letter to each square, to form four ordinary words.

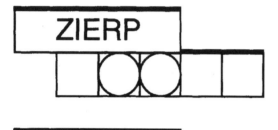

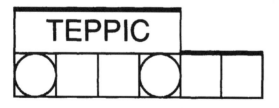

ZIERP

TOQUA

PHONYT

TEPPIC

A CITIZEN TURNS INTO THIS AT TAX TIME.

Now arrange the circled letters to form the surprise answer, as suggested by the above cartoon.

Print answer here **A** " ___ - ______ "

JUMBLE®

Unscramble these four Jumbles, one letter to each square, to form four ordinary words.

BEIPD

KAYLB

THEIRZ

TADEEB

She must be exhausted
Puff puff

THIS WAS DRAWN AFTER HER FAST-PACED DANCE SCENE.

Now arrange the circled letters to form the surprise answer, as suggested by the above cartoon.

Print answer here A

JUMBLE®

Unscramble these four Jumbles, one letter to each square, to form four ordinary words.

WETIC

RETEX

STIDGE

CHIANG

OW
WHAT THE PLUMBER DID TO HIS SHOULDER.

Now arrange the circled letters to form the surprise answer, as suggested by the above cartoon.

Print answer here " "

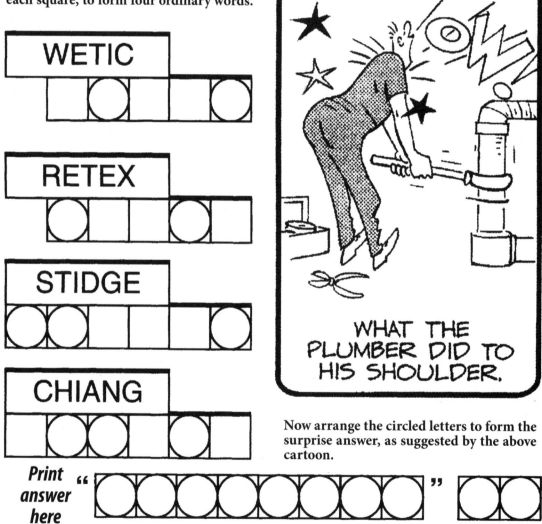

PUZZLE 139

JUMBLE®

Unscramble these four Jumbles, one letter to each square, to form four ordinary words.

COLIG

LOFEN

ZURQAT

DEXENP

We need more practice
Really?
LETTING HIS PARTNER FALL DID THIS TO THEIR RELATIONSHIP.

Now arrange the circled letters to form the surprise answer, as suggested by the above cartoon.

Print answer here ○○○ IT ○○ ○○○○

PUZZLE 140

JUMBLE®

Unscramble these four Jumbles, one letter to each square, to form four ordinary words.

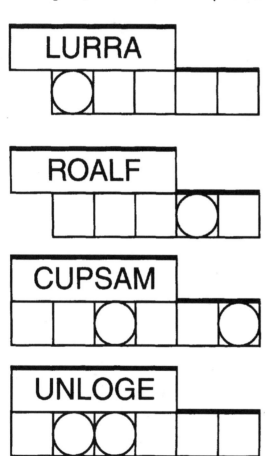

LURRA

ROALF

CUPSAM

UNLOGE

Let's split the salad, Agatha
I hear that Mabel is ...

WHAT THE GOS-SIPS ENJOYED SHARING AT THEIR LUNCH.

Now arrange the circled letters to form the surprise answer, as suggested by the above cartoon.

Print answer here

JUMBLE®

Unscramble these four Jumbles, one letter to each square, to form four ordinary words.

NEMOD

FEYHT

IVIDDE

GLARAN

Now arrange the circled letters to form the surprise answer, as suggested by the above cartoon.

Print answer here ☐☐ ☐☐☐☐ HIS ☐☐☐☐

PUZZLE 142

JUMBLE®

Unscramble these four Jumbles, one letter to each square, to form four ordinary words.

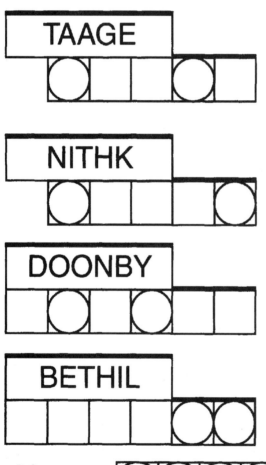

TAAGE

NITHK

DOONBY

BETHIL

My flat is freezing
No rent 'til I'm warm

WHAT THE JANITOR DID WHEN THE FURNACE FAILED.

Now arrange the circled letters to form the surprise answer, as suggested by the above cartoon.

Print answer here ○○○○ THE "○○○○○"

PUZZLE 143

JUMBLE®

Unscramble these four Jumbles, one letter to each square, to form four ordinary words.

NYLOP

KEVAN

VAJILO

DEAMOP

Ouch, I thought it was open
EASY TO GET WALKING INTO A GLASS DOOR.

Now arrange the circled letters to form the surprise answer, as suggested by the above cartoon.

Print answer here A

JUMBLE®

Unscramble these four Jumbles, one letter to each square, to form four ordinary words.

JUTSO

FOIMT

REMORT

SCUABA

Long way from shore
WHAT THE HIPPIE SAID WHEN HE WENT ON AN OCEAN CRUISE.

Now arrange the circled letters to form the surprise answer, as suggested by the above cartoon.

Print answer here “ ”

PUZZLE 145

JUMBLE®

Unscramble these four Jumbles, one letter to each square, to form four ordinary words.

CUIMS

YOANN

GINANA

TEMRIP

They'll do anything for votes
WHAT THE CANDIDATES BECAME WHEN THEY JOINED THE PICNIC RACE.

Now arrange the circled letters to form the surprise answer, as suggested by the above cartoon.

Print answer here

JUMBLE®

Unscramble these four Jumbles, one letter to each square, to form four ordinary words.

CADEY

SLURY

BENAMO

ASANUE

The bills are paid, and we're still on our feet
WHAT A STEADY INCOME WILL LET YOU KEEP.

Now arrange the circled letters to form the surprise answer, as suggested by the above cartoon.

Print answer here

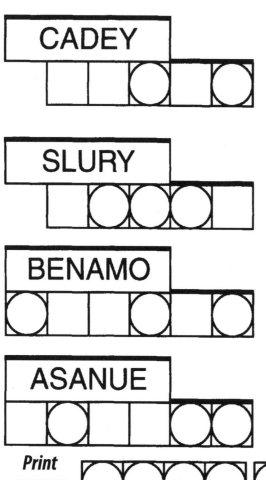

PUZZLE 147

JUMBLE®

Unscramble these four Jumbles, one letter to each square, to form four ordinary words.

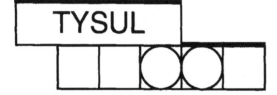

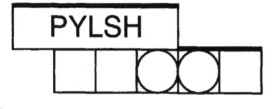

PYLSH

TYSUL

FLEEBE

NOSPER

A GOOD THING FOR A TIRED WITCH TO DO.

Now arrange the circled letters to form the surprise answer, as suggested by the above cartoon.

Print answer here A " "

PUZZLE

148

JUMBLE®

Unscramble these four Jumbles, one letter to each square, to form four ordinary words.

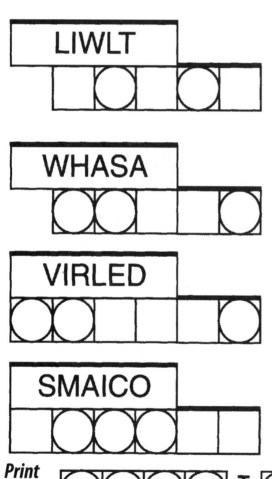

LIWLT

WHASA

VIRLED

SMAICO

PAYING FOR A GOURMET DINNER CAN BE THIS.

Now arrange the circled letters to form the surprise answer, as suggested by the above cartoon.

Print answer here TO

PUZZLE 149

JUMBLE®

Unscramble these four Jumbles, one letter to each square, to form four ordinary words.

HINSY

ABDEK

REYMOB

BLUMJE

I see you, Bobby
FINAL EXAM
WHY THE MATH STUDENT COULDN'T FOOL THE INSTRUCTOR.

Now arrange the circled letters to form the surprise answer, as suggested by the above cartoon.

Print answer here HE ◯◯◯ HIS ◯◯◯◯◯◯

JUMBLE®

Unscramble these four Jumbles, one letter to each square, to form four ordinary words.

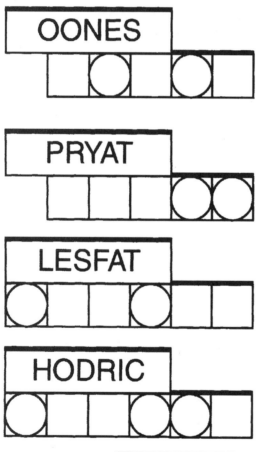

OONES

PRYAT

LESFAT

HODRIC

Where were you yesterday?
I called. Nobody answered
THE TRANSMISSION MAN WAS FIRED BECAUSE HE WAS ---

Now arrange the circled letters to form the surprise answer, as suggested by the above cartoon.

Print answer here “ ”

PUZZLE 151

JUMBLE®

Unscramble these four Jumbles, one letter to each square, to form four ordinary words.

DUILF

GUZAE

EMPAND

YALAWY

You do these
And you get those
HOW THE BOSS HANDLED THE HEAVY WORKLOAD.

Now arrange the circled letters to form the surprise answer, as suggested by the above cartoon.

Print answer here HE " "

PUZZLE 152

JUMBLE®

Unscramble these four Jumbles, one letter to each square, to form four ordinary words.

POTVI

MUTON

TENAGE

HABINS

Knew it all the time
WHAT KIND OF CASE WAS IT FOR THE WHODUNIT ADDICT?

Now arrange the circled letters to form the surprise answer, as suggested by the above cartoon.

Print answer here ____ **AND** _____

PUZZLE 153

JUMBLE®

Unscramble these four Jumbles, one letter to each square, to form four ordinary words.

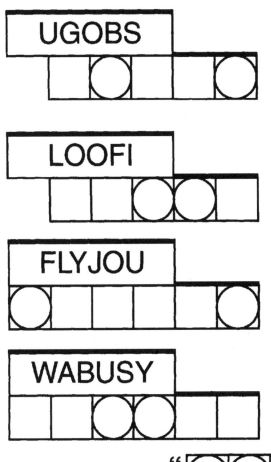

UGOBS

LOOFI

FLYJOU

WABUSY

We'll get a good price when they get fat

FOR A FARMER, FEEDING THE PIGS IS THIS.

Now arrange the circled letters to form the surprise answer, as suggested by the above cartoon.

Print answer here A “   ”

PUZZLE 154

JUMBLE®

Unscramble these four Jumbles, one letter to each square, to form four ordinary words.

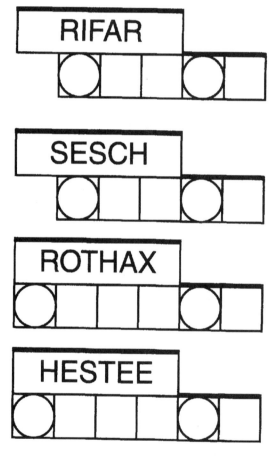

RIFAR

SESCH

ROTHAX

HESTEE

There goes my last ten bucks

TOUGH TO GET OUT OF A SLOW HORSE.

Now arrange the circled letters to form the surprise answer, as suggested by the above cartoon.

Print answer here

JUMBLE®

Unscramble these four Jumbles, one letter to each square, to form four ordinary words.

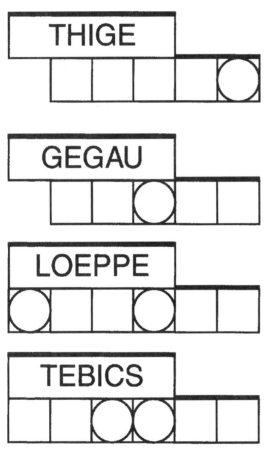

THIGE

GEGAU

LOEPPE

TEBICS

A SPEEDY WAY TO BUILD A STAIRCASE.

Now arrange the circled letters to form the surprise answer, as suggested by the above cartoon.

Print answer here ◯◯◯◯ IT ◯◯

PUZZLE 156

JUMBLE®

Unscramble these four Jumbles, one letter to each square, to form four ordinary words.

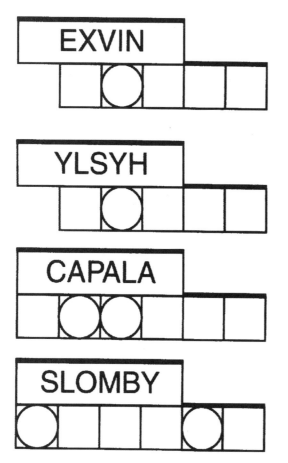

EXVIN

YLSYH

CAPALA

SLOMBY

WHAT THE "WELL-DRESSED" GENTLEMAN WITH SCUFFED SHOES LACKED.

Now arrange the circled letters to form the surprise answer, as suggested by the above cartoon.

Print answer here

PUZZLE 157

JUMBLE®

Unscramble these four Jumbles, one letter to each square, to form four ordinary words.

YATTS

TYDIT

RAZDAH

LOVVEE

Sorry, boss, the front stalled
WOOF
FORTY DEGREES WARMER THAN FORE-CAST PUT THE WEATHERMAN HERE.

Now arrange the circled letters to form the surprise answer, as suggested by the above cartoon.

Print answer here THE " "

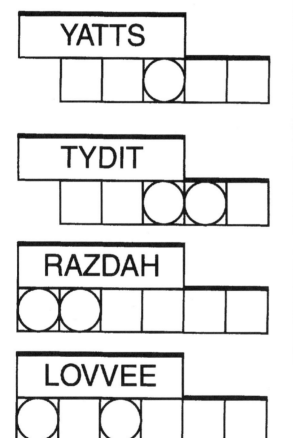

PUZZLE
158

JUMBLE®

Unscramble these four Jumbles, one letter to each square, to form four ordinary words.

TARIE

HAADE

REALYY

STIFIM

WHY GRANDMA PUT UP PICKLES EVERY YEAR.

Now arrange the circled letters to form the surprise answer, as suggested by the above cartoon.

Print answer here **SHE**

PUZZLE 159

JUMBLE®

Unscramble these four Jumbles, one letter to each square, to form four ordinary words.

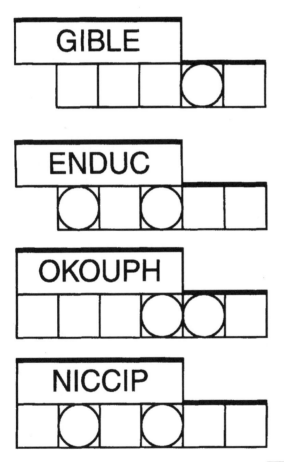

GIBLE

ENDUC

OKOUPH

NICCIP

WHAT THE COACH ENJOYED WITH HIS MORNING COFFEE.

Now arrange the circled letters to form the surprise answer, as suggested by the above cartoon.

Print answer here

JUMBLE®

Unscramble these four Jumbles, one letter to each square, to form four ordinary words.

PIRRO

BOSEE

LOVEUM

SMARDI

Outstanding quality
THE PRINTER GOT A RAISE BECAUSE HIS WORK WAS THIS.

Now arrange the circled letters to form the surprise answer, as suggested by the above cartoon.

Print answer here

JUMBLE®

Explosion

CHALLENGER PUZZLES

PUZZLE 161

JUMBLE®

Unscramble these six Jumbles, one letter to each square, to form six ordinary words.

NORREC

LEESAW

PURBAT

YUPRIF

LYKING

SARGYS

This is it. From now on I'll use cash
WHAT THE DOC-TOR RESORTED TO WHEN THE CREDIT CHARGES GOT TOO HIGH.

Now arrange the circled letters to form the surprise answer, as suggested by the above cartoon.

Print answer here

" ○○○○○○○ " ○○○○○○○

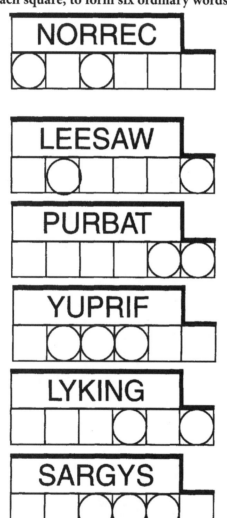

JUMBLE®

Unscramble these six Jumbles, one letter to each square, to form six ordinary words.

WALLUF

NUCKOL

ODUXTE

BONBBI

REPHOG

LARROP

Just a little bit higher, no lower
THE TAILOR HAD TROUBLE WITH THE WRESTLER BECAUSE HE WAS ---

Now arrange the circled letters to form the surprise answer, as suggested by the above cartoon.

Print answer here

TO

JUMBLE®

Unscramble these six Jumbles, one letter to each square, to form six ordinary words.

CAMBEL

REGOUM

HAWLIE

SCARFA

PRAILL

GONBEE

He never stops talking
English
THE VENTRILO-QUIST SAID HIS DUMMY WAS THIS.

Now arrange the circled letters to form the surprise answer, as suggested by the above cartoon.

Print answer here

A ○○○○○○ OF "○○○○○○"

JUMBLE®

Unscramble these six Jumbles, one letter to each square, to form six ordinary words.

TUNBOT

DUIMBE

ENGERE

DYRAMI

HYSERR

LIMNAR

No phones, no reports, hot sun, nice tan
THE OFFICE WORKER YEARNED FOR A DAY AT THE BEACH BECAUSE SHE HAD ---

Now arrange the circled letters to form the surprise answer, as suggested by the above cartoon.

Print answer here

A " ◯◯◯◯◯◯◯ " ◯◯◯◯◯◯◯

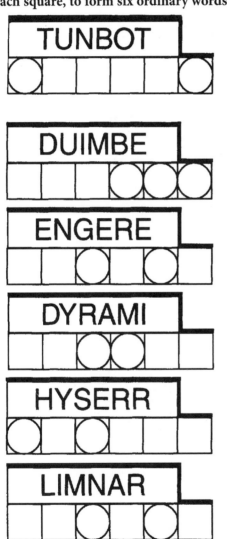

PUZZLE 165

JUMBLE®

Unscramble these six Jumbles, one letter to each square, to form six ordinary words.

UNMEBB

NURTUE

ENTHIZ

ROMMIE

MEEGUL

GOTSDY

How come I get all the work?
OK, give me some from your pile
HOW DID THE TAILORS SETTLE THEIR DIFFER-ENCES?

Now arrange the circled letters to form the surprise answer, as suggested by the above cartoon.

Print answer here

"○○○○○○" ○○○○ ○○○

PUZZLE 166

JUMBLE®

Unscrambled these six Jumbles, one letter to each square, to form six ordinary words.

GOHMEA

AXNYRL

STRAIG

UNCHAP

BEFILE

WIMDLE

Gosh, Mom, you sure make it sparkle
WHAT MOM BECAME WHEN SHE POLISHED THE SILVERWARE.

Now arrange the circled letters to form the surprise answer, as suggested by the above cartoon.

Print answer here

A " "

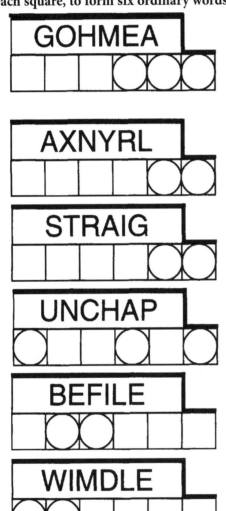

PUZZLE 167

JUMBLE®

Unscramble these six Jumbles, one letter to each square, to form six ordinary words.

YOMPLE

EXGONY

NORIPS

HURGOT

PLECOM

LEFTLI

How do I love thee ...
The words are so beautiful
WHEN HIS PROSE BROUGHT TEARS TO HER EYES, SHE SAID IT WAS ---

Now arrange the circled letters to form the surprise answer, as suggested by the above cartoon.

Print answer here

PUZZLE 168

JUMBLE®

Unscramble these six Jumbles, one letter to each square, to form six ordinary words.

WHARKE

CLUBEK

EECDAC

BALIVE

DYLOUB

FOTEEF

We're transferring you to submarine duty, Jones
D

WHERE THE SAILOR ENDED UP WHEN HE FAILED THE EXAM.

Now arrange the circled letters to form the surprise answer, as suggested by the above cartoon.

Print answer here

“ ”

PUZZLE 169

JUMBLE®

Unscramble these six Jumbles, one letter to each square, to form six ordinary words.

BROBRE

IMSURT

MEEBAC

CENTEM

OPTECK

NOCABE

Wonderful for relaxing
He has a string of stores
SELLING FOOTSTOOLS TURNED INTO THIS.

Now arrange the circled letters to form the surprise answer, as suggested by the above cartoon.

Print answer here

AN

JUMBLE®

Unscramble these six Jumbles, one letter to each square, to form six ordinary words.

SUTHPY

LISGRY

SPELTE

DINKAP

SELAMY

NORGAD

I couldn't make it with the pen
That's where you're going, Shakespeare
WHY DID THE MISGUIDED POET TURN TO CRIME?

Now arrange the circled letters to form the surprise answer, as suggested by the above cartoon.

Print answer here

PUZZLE 171

JUMBLE®

Unscramble these six Jumbles, one letter to each square, to form six ordinary words.

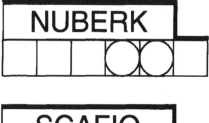

NUBERK

SCAFIO

SHAPIR

JOOSUY

STOFRY

HUBBYC

I can use a drink
WHAT HE NEEDED WHEN HE GOT THE BILL FOR CAR REPAIRS.

Now arrange the circled letters to form the surprise answer, as suggested by the above cartoon.

Print answer here

A

PUZZLE 172

JUMBLE®

Unscramble these six Jumbles, one letter to each square, to form six ordinary words.

BELBUB

RELPHE

WEDOMA

RAMAAD

SERJEY

CLEFEE

Nobody can beat my prices
He jumps from one company to the other

WHAT HE BECAME WHEN HE BOUGHT THE TIRE BUSINESS.

Now arrange the circled letters to form the surprise answer, as suggested by the above cartoon.

Print answer here

A “ ”

PUZZLE 173

JUMBLE®

Unscramble these six Jumbles, one letter to each square, to form six ordinary words.

THENUR

APTECK

TRIUNA

YURCOT

REMIPE

REFILP

It looks like a beautiful painting
Wonderful composition
THE PHOTOGRAPHER WON THE AWARD BE-CAUSE HIS WORK WAS ---

Now arrange the circled letters to form the surprise answer, as suggested by the above cartoon.

Print answer here

JUMBLE®

Unscramble these six Jumbles, one letter to each square, to form six ordinary words.

SUSTLY

CHYSIP

URAUBE

NAANAB

CONARY

GURDIT

Great tones and saved $300
WHAT HE ENDED UP WITH WHEN HE BOUGHT THE STEREO ON SALE.

Now arrange the circled letters to form the surprise answer, as suggested by the above cartoon.

Print answer here

A " "

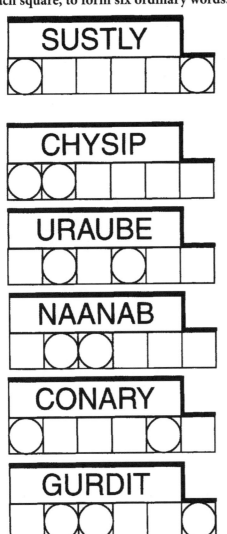

PUZZLE 175

JUMBLE®

Unscramble these six Jumbles, one letter to each square, to form six ordinary words.

INGINN

FIFRAM

BORRAH

RAMPHE

TRAUGI

DAMTLE

WHAT HER BRIDGE PARTNER BECAME WHEN SHE WON THE BID.

Now arrange the circled letters to form the surprise answer, as suggested by the above cartoon.

Print answer here

A " ◯◯◯◯◯ ◯◯◯◯◯ " ◯◯◯

PUZZLE 176

JUMBLE®

Unscramble these six Jumbles, one letter to each square, to form six ordinary words.

CHARNB

LOONED

NYWIRT

CUGATH

WAHGIE

BRAYNE

That didn't play long
LAST DAY
WHEN THE CRITICS PANNED THE TORNADO MOVIE, IT WAS---

Now arrange the circled letters to form the surprise answer, as suggested by the above cartoon.

Print answer here

THE

PUZZLE 177

JUMBLE®

Unscramble these six Jumbles, one letter to each square, to form six ordinary words.

EXCOBI

ROSABB

DELAUF

EMBLUH

FLIECK

YURETS

Hey, that's my seat
No, it's mine
Let's try the anthem

WHAT THE STUDENT ORCHESTRA ENDED UP PLAYING.

Now arrange the circled letters to form the surprise answer, as suggested by the above cartoon.

Print answer here

JUMBLE®

Unscramble these six Jumbles, one letter to each square, to form six ordinary words.

NUTBOY

BLACOT

YORRAS

ENBODY

TRAVOC

DUNBOA

This is too frustrating
JUNIOR STOPPED PLAYING WITH THE MARIONETTE BE-CAUSE HE---

Now arrange the circled letters to form the surprise answer, as suggested by the above cartoon.

Print answer here

______'_ "_____" IT

PUZZLE 179

JUMBLE®

Unscramble these six Jumbles, one letter to each square, to form six ordinary words.

DYLGOO

DELBEH

DETHOB

TOOMIN

RETOAT

RABIUL

...and don't move until we land
WHAT MOM DID WHEN THE KIDS GOT ROWDY IN THE AIR.

Now arrange the circled letters to form the surprise answer, as suggested by the above cartoon.

Print answer here

“ ”

JUMBLE®

Unscramble these six Jumbles, one letter to each square, to form six ordinary words.

ENIAMA

SNUFIO

DEYMEL

CLAJEO

SMURTE

ONASAT

Full house. We'll make a buck tonight

ENJOYED BY THE JAZZ QUARTET WHEN THE CLUB WAS SOLD OUT.

Now arrange the circled letters to form the surprise answer, as suggested by the above cartoon.

Print answer here

A " "

Answers

1. **Jumbles:** EXACT CREEL ASSURE POLICY
Answer: The most brutal part of that heavyweight fight—THE PRICE OF THE SEATS
2. **Jumbles:** PENCE VIGIL GIBLET EVOLVE
Answer: The hardest thing to give is—TO GIVE IN
3. **Jumbles:** ADAGE EMERY SLEEPY MUSTER
Answer: What that wild-animal trainer at the circus does—"TAMES" TO PLEASE
4. **Jumbles:** ELITE HEDGE LAWFUL THROAT
Answer: That letter made ill will—THE LETTER "W"
5. **Jumbles:** SNOWY BEFOG SCHEME RELISH
Answer: What horsepower should be mixed with—HORSE SENSE
6. **Jumbles:** IMBUE FLORA WEASEL DOUBLY
Answer: What those newly hatched termites were—BABES IN THE WOOD
7. **Jumbles:** HAVEN NATAL ALBINO ELDEST
Answer: That unconvincing witness was making the jury wonder—WHAT "LIES" AHEAD
8. **Jumbles:** ELOPE LIBEL FILLET BUTANE
Answer: What you wouldn't expect a vegetarian to do when the food is unsatisfactory—BEEF ABOUT IT
9. **Jumbles:** APRON FUROR CUDDLE BECALM
Answer: What that quarreling acting team always did just before going on stage—"MADE UP"
10. **Jumbles:** FAVOR BISON WHOLLY MAGNUM
Answer: What that bashful wallflower was hoping to do with the man of her choice—GROW ON HIM
11. **Jumbles:** ELATE CIVIL TUMULT DETAIN
Answer: What a siesta is—A MATINEE "IDLE"
12. **Jumbles:** OPIUM GLOAT DINGHY COBALT
Answer: A guy who tries to start a business on a shoestring sometimes ends up taking this—A GOOD LACING
13. **Jumbles:** BRAVE ERASE UNPAID CLOUDY
Answer: When you call the plumber because of a leak, it might end up being this—A "DRAIN" ON YOU
14. **Jumbles:** NEEDY BARON SECEDE ELDEST
Answer: The judge's words were less important than this—HIS SENTENCES
15. **Jumbles:** PROVE SHEEP INFUSE MANIAC
Answer: What an employee has if he laughs at the boss's jokes even when they make no this—"SENSE"
16. **Jumbles:** OAKEN FAITH PREACH CUPFUL
Answer: Could be a head covering for a traveler to the Arctic—A POLAR ICE "CAP"
17. **Jumbles:** GRAIN ITCHY MELODY VASSAL
Answer: What happened when their shellfish business suffered financial reverses?—IT WAS A "CLAM-ITY" (calamity)
18. **Jumbles:** MOUTH FEVER PSYCHE UPLIFT
Answer: What the taxidermist's personality certainly was—STUFFY
19. **Jumbles:** METAL CUBIT SHADOW KILLER
Answer: What he would do every time he saw the girl at the candy counter—SWEET-TALK HER
20. **Jumbles:** CLEFT BRIBE DEFILE INTACT
Answer: The egotist's love letter—THE LETTER "I"
21. **Jumbles:** GROIN DINER COERCE FIESTA
Answer: When the skunk entered the room, it got attention because it was this—THE "SCENTER" OF IT
22. **Jumbles:** WOMEN PANSY CORNEA BICKER
Answer: Where the deposits are "frozen assets"—IN A "SNOW BANK"
23. **Jumbles:** ELATE MINUS SPLEEN NUDISM
Answer: The nervous tailor was always on this—PINS & NEEDLES
24. **Jumbles:** IVORY FIORD SHANTY DEFACE
Answer: That well-dressed woman was indeed a credit to her husband, thanks to this—HIS CREDIT
25. **Jumbles:** REARM EMERY BEHOLD STODGY
Answer: A comfortable old shoe might be this, through thick and thin—YOUR "SOLE" MATE
26. **Jumbles:** AUDIT EXPEL BICEPS UNLOAD
Answer: When gossip is at its most malicious, they sometimes relish it as this—"DELICIOUS"
27. **Jumbles:** CEASE FLOUR RARELY INFIRM
Answer: The curve that usually sets things straight—A SMILE
28. **Jumbles:** GUEST PLUSH SURELY IRONIC
Answer: What a crooked politician with a "knotty" problem might try to do—PULL STRINGS
29. **Jumbles:** AORTA BUILT MALADY FILLET
Answer: Words of praise that seldom fall flat—FLATTERY
30. **Jumbles:** EXERT FACET QUORUM TURNIP
Answer: Why you should study the history of the past—THERE'S A FUTURE IN IT
31. **Jumbles:** BEGUN JADED SKEWER NICELY
Answer: What a green thumb can mean for a professional gardener—"GREENBACKS"
32. **Jumbles:** CURVE BERTH ENZYME HARROW
Answer: What the male sheep shouted in order to get his mate's attention—"HEY, EWE"
33. **Jumbles:** HUSKY CAMEO JOYFUL HEALTH
Answer: When a coward gets into a "jam," you can expect him to do this—SHAKE LIKE JELLY
34. **Jumbles:** FOIST CHAMP SNUGLY MYSTIC
Answer: What the misogynist felt he had in the world—A "MISS-SHUN"
35. **Jumbles:** ABASH HYENA SWIVEL DAMASK
Answer: Strong lungs often appeal to people with this—WEAK HEADS
36. **Jumbles:** ABBEY CHOKE VOLUME GUTTER
Answer: Age may be the difference between these—A BULGE & A CURVE
37. **Jumbles:** GNARL PRONE LIKELY TRUDGE
Answer: A guy who has the right aim in life sometimes fails to do this, figuratively—"PULL THE TRIGGER"
38. **Jumbles:** STUNG CURRY FARINA JURIST
Answer: What kind of an experience was it for the jinni to be in that bottle—A JARRING ONE
39. **Jumbles:** BLANK MACAW CABANA WINTRY
Answer: What the college halfback was in his studies—WAY BACK
40. **Jumbles:** DOWDY JOKER ASYLUM BEAUTY
Answer: She had a steady job trying to keep him at this—A STEADY JOB
41. **Jumbles:** SUAVE ABIDE KITTEN HARBOR
Answer: A gold digger is one who has what it takes to do this—TAKE WHAT ONE HAS
42. **Jumbles:** YODEL PORGY UNLIKE OBJECT
Answer: Could be a skeptic's outlook—A "DOUBT LOOK"
43. **Jumbles:** YOKEL KHAKI ENMITY CONVEX
Answer: The only voice that Dad sometimes has in family affairs—"INVOICE"
44. **Jumbles:** BURST LIMIT MOSAIC TOFFEE
Answer: What Dracula got when he mistook a snowman for a human being—FROSTBITE
45. **Jumbles:** BRAVO DITTY INTENT TURTLE
Answer: What to pay if you don't want to spend too much—ATTENTION
46. **Jumbles:** FILMY QUEST MURMUR BUSHEL
Answer: He deserves to do this when he behaves like a worm—SQUIRM

47. **Jumbles:** HENNA JINGO INDICT POPLIN
Answer: For him, nothing was so difficult as doing this—NOTHING

48. **Jumbles:** TAWNY VISTA RADIUM POWDER
Answer: The best way to make a long story short—INTERRUPT

49. **Jumbles:** FLOUT WAGER UNPACK CALICO
Answer: Ignorance of the law is no excuse, especially if you're this—A KNOW-IT-ALL

50. **Jumbles:** DROOP KETCH CAUCUS ENTICE
Answer: Some people think that a kid with too much spunk might benefit from a little of this—SPANK

51. **Jumbles:** GUMMY SMACK BEAVER CORRAL
Answer: The best labor-saving device—A LEGACY

52. **Jumbles:** SAVOR RUMMY SADIST RATIFY
Answer: Some say that if you marry a widow you won't do this—MARRY "A-MISS"

53. **Jumbles:** SCARF PUPIL JUNKET SUBDUE
Answer: What the teacher did when the antelope took his final exam—PASSED THE BUCK

54. **Jumbles:** MONEY CROUP SCURVY METRIC
Answer: What the swindler's posture was—IMPOSTURE

55. **Jumbles:** HOVEL MOTIF AGENDA ELIXER
Answer: A jury never works right when it's this—"FIXED"

56. **Jumbles:** HARPY SUITE BESIDE RECTOR
Answer: What some people's handwriting is—A "SCRIPT" TEASE

57. **Jumbles:** PHONY SCOUT MUFFLE GULLET
Answer: Where's the fencing master?—OUT TO "LUNGE"

58. **Jumbles:** BYLAW MADLY CHERUB FLORAL
Answer: What they thought it was when the wimp tried to act like a wolf—A "HOWL"

59. **Jumbles:** WHINE SYLPH JUSTLY QUARRY
Answer: What the stand-up comedian equips himself with—QUIPS

60. **Jumbles:** TESTY RAJAH HALLOW SPEEDY
Answer: Could this be another name for that health club?—THE SWEAT SHOP

61. **Jumbles:** IRONY SCOUT WHOLLY BONNET
Answer: What the self-centered trumpet player liked to do—TOOT HIS OWN HORN

62. **Jumbles:** GUARD VAPOR DURESS SECEDE
Answer: Where the women officers enjoyed going while off duty—TO A DRESS PARADE

63. **Jumbles:** ALBUM FAINT KIMONO JUMPER
Answer: What the postman delivered to the Chinese vessel—JUNK MAIL

64. **Jumbles:** POUND VALET SLUICE TALKER
Answer: Why the botanist bought the factories—HE LIKED "PLANTS"

65. **Jumbles:** FIFTY AGENT VERMIN FARINA
Answer: What the crooked politician wanted the whistle-stop tour to turn into—THE GRAVY TRAIN

66. **Jumbles:** PEACE PUTTY UNSAID TRIPLE
Answer: An off-color joke made them do this—TURN PALE

67. **Jumbles:** GLAND CRAWL UPKEEP UPROAR
Answer: What the knife sharpener considered his job—"DULL" WORK

68. **Jumbles:** DRAWL PRUNE INLAID LETHAL
Answer: A good thing to hold onto when taking a flight—THE HANDRAIL

69. **Jumbles:** SHOWY HENNA NOVICE MENACE
Answer: Too many of these can make you sick on a cruise—OCEAN WAVES

70. **Jumbles:** BRIAR ADAPT MINGLE FALLEN
Answer: How the student manicurist did on her exam—SHE "NAILED" IT

71. **Jumbles:** BASIS ABATE VASSAL PANTRY
Answer: Always kept by a restaurant owner—TABS ON THE TABS

72. **Jumbles:** CHAOS LATHE DISCUS CROTCH
Answer: Good students at a barber college will do this—CUT A CLASS

73. **Jumbles:** TIGER SUITE INVENT REDUCE
Answer: What the customer considered the loan rate—"INTEREST-ING"

74. **Jumbles:** COLIC OCTET KERNEL DEVOUR
Answer: This happened to his work at the scenic canyon—HE "OVERLOOKED" IT

75. **Jumbles:** JUICE CROUP CLOTHE SHAKEN
Answer: The first thing the ex-boxer was asked to do in his new job—PUNCH THE CLOCK

76. **Jumbles:** DOGMA WRATH OUTLAW USEFUL
Answer: The sleepy farmer responded to the rooster with this—"FOWL" WORDS

77. **Jumbles:** HOVEL BERET OPAQUE INDIGO
Answer: What she showed her obnoxious date—THE DOOR

78. **Jumbles:** GNOME DALLY STUPID CLAUSE
Answer: What kind of humorist was the comic?—A "STAND-UP" GUY

79. **Jumbles:** MINCE BLOAT LAWYER UNHOLY
Answer: The tightrope walker hired the accountant because he knew—HOW TO BALANCE

80. **Jumbles:** EPOCH LISLE PARDON SUBDUE
Answer: What the polo player did when the bill came for the drinks—"PONIED" UP

81. **Jumbles:** FLUTE VENOM RADISH FUTURE
Answer: What Fido enjoyed as the family finished dinner—"LEFT-UNDERS"

82. **Jumbles:** CLUCK DIRTY MODERN CALLOW
Answer: Drilling for oil is always this—"CRUDE" WORK

83. **Jumbles:** FORGO QUAKE BLUING SHREWD
Answer: What the dentist admired on his road trip—THE BRIDGE WORK

84. **Jumbles:** ABBEY JUMPY TIPTOE FETISH
Answer: Does it take a lot to use a brace?—JUST A "BIT"

85. **Jumbles:** BERTH MOUSY LOCKET PEWTER
Answer: What it takes to train a thoroughbred—A WORK HORSE

86. **Jumbles:** PEONY ENSUE GOATEE JACKAL
Answer: The freeloader's favorite dessert—"SPONGE" CAKE

87. **Jumbles:** TRACT BATCH CHORUS UPTOWN
Answer: What the designer said when the garment was done—THAT'S A "WRAP"

88. **Jumbles:** QUILT TEASE QUARRY FELONY
Answer: Sure to be this after a night on the town—SURLY EARLY

89. **Jumbles:** KNACK GOURD ZODIAC VERBAL
Answer: Fixing the kitchen sink left Pop like this—"DRAINED"

90. **Jumbles:** JETTY LINEN OCELOT UNLOAD
Answer: The census taker was hired because he could—BE COUNTED ON

91. **Jumbles:** EXCEL MILKY DREDGE ASSAIL
Answer: When he arrived for the hunt he was—DRESSED TO "KILL"

92. **Jumbles:** SWISH GRIPE VALISE FINITE
Answer: What a crash diet can lead to—"FAST" LIVING

93. **Jumbles:** NOBLE RIGOR NAUGHT PELVIS
Answer: What Mom came up with when the carpet was mysteriously stained—A "SOLUTION"

94. **Jumbles:** EAGLE GLEAM LAGOON THRASH
Answer: Served by the aspiring actor at the breakfast counter—"HAM" AND EGGS

95. **Jumbles:** MIRTH MUSTY SQUIRM UNLIKE
Answer: What Mom created when she used her new mixer—QUITE A STIR

96. **Jumbles:** NOISE GUIDE SNAPPY STRONG
Answer: What the customer experienced when he visited the new pub—A GRAND "OPENING"

97. **Jumbles:** PLUME VALVE MALICE ENDURE
Answer: When he was awakened early, his wife was—ALARMED

98. **Jumbles:** SNARL POISE GHETTO CARNAL
Answer: What the kids turned Dad's van into—A "SPORTS" CAR

99. **Jumbles:** BRAWL AWFUL BUMPER DECEIT
Answer: How the lioness felt when surrounded by her cubs—FULL OF "PRIDE"

100. **Jumbles:** BORAX SOUSE PREFIX TIDBIT
Answer: What she did when she received a necklace from the pirate chest—"TREASURED" IT

101. **Jumbles:** FANCY HELLO SAVORY GAMBIT
Answer: What the computer staff considered the break lounge—A CHAT ROOM

102. **Jumbles:** REBEL SNOWY DELUGE GARISH
Answer: When the students got unruly, the art teacher did this—HE DREW THE LINE

103. **Jumbles:** TESTY PAPER TRICKY NINETY
Answer: What she gave him after her spill at the skating rink—AN "ICY" STARE

104. **Jumbles:** HITCH AIDED PETITE AROUSE
Answer: A conversation at a sports bar can become this—"SPIRITED"

105. **Jumbles:** PILOT EMPTY SAVAGE SATIRE
Answer: Why Junior didn't get any supper—IT WAS PAST REPAST

106. **Jumbles:** MOOSE LLAMA PULPIT EYELET
Answer: What the dentist and the mayor shared—LOTS OF "PULL"

107. **Jumbles:** CHIDE FINAL SWIVEL NATURE
Answer: To be successful, a clothing retailer must always be—WELL-SUITED

108. **Jumbles:** CRIME BYLAW BIGAMY BABOON
Answer: What he took when he ran across the street—A "GAMBOL"

109. **Jumbles:** QUAIL CHALK PENURY UPWARD
Answer: What the pool player wanted to do—RACK UP A WIN

110. **Jumbles:** FOIST FLOUR ARMORY TRUDGE
Answer: Nobody is surprised when "dormitory" is turned into this—DIRTY ROOM

111. **Jumbles:** WAFER VAGUE RELISH TWINGE
Answer: What he did when the ceiling fan needed repair—GAVE IT A WHIRL

112. **Jumbles:** BLAZE PROVE POWDER BALLET
Answer: What the hairdresser did when the customer got nasty—BLEW HER TOP

113. **Jumbles:** LURID DUCAT CARBON HANDLE
Answer: This resulted when the Frenchman didn't say good-bye—ADO OVER ADIEU

114. **Jumbles:** UNIFY IVORY SOLACE FERRET
Answer: What the careful robbers sought for their getaway—A "SAFE" ROUTE

115. **Jumbles:** CHAFE BEGUN ABSURD SQUALL
Answer: The comedy contestant was so bad, they said his routine was—"LAUGHABLE"

116. **Jumbles:** ODDLY CUBIT HEARTH WIDEST
Answer: What the cook did when the server dropped the tray—"DISHED" IT OUT

117. **Jumbles:** CLOTH BRAIN AVENUE ZIGZAG
Answer: Too much beer can lead to this—A "HANG OVER"

118. **Jumbles:** CHIME ACUTE BEFALL SOIREE
Answer: What she gave her boyfriend for his birthday—A "BEAU" TIE

119. **Jumbles:** ERASE PLUSH LOCATE INFUSE
Answer: For many, skiing turns winter into this—THE "FALL" SEASON

120. **Jumbles:** SHEEP NOVEL THIRTY SIPHON
Answer: Often exercised by a successful executive—HIS OPTIONS

121. **Jumbles:** BATON CHANT MISERY SYSTEM
Answer: What she took to appear in the horror movie—A "SCREAM" TEST

122. **Jumbles:** CRESS ENVOY NEPHEW FALLOW
Answer: A tailor's business is usually this—ONLY SEW SEW

123. **Jumbles:** HUMID EVENT CRABBY LUNACY
Answer: How he drove down the fairway—IN A CART

124. **Jumbles:** PUPIL CLOVE TALLOW NICETY
Answer: What it took to get him to the altar—A LITTLE "WILE"

125. **Jumbles:** WEDGE MAJOR NOZZLE GLOOMY
Answer: The farmer wanted to see this—HIS MONEY GROW

126. **Jumbles:** CURRY SHAKY UNCOIL HUMBLE
Answer: What he pushed when he ran out of gas—HIS LUCK

127. **Jumbles:** BRAVE INKED UNRULY FAMILY
Answer: To a mechanic, coffee is often this—"BREAK" FLUID

128. **Jumbles:** DOUSE PLAIT EMBODY QUORUM
Answer: What the reasonable fortune-teller charged—"MEDIUM" RATES

129. **Jumbles:** OFTEN SNORT JOSTLE OPIATE
Answer: It takes this to become a successful banker—LOTS OF INTEREST

130. **Jumbles:** PECAN TOKEN EXTANT IMPACT
Answer: Preparing an annual return can do this—TAX PATIENCE

131. **Jumbles:** APRON CYCLE ESTATE ERMINE
Answer: What one out of ten cows is—TEN PERCENT

132. **Jumbles:** LEECH EXILE SUNDAE POLISH
Answer: Where the queen was often seen—IN "HI" PLACES

133. **Jumbles:** LADLE CHOKE RACIAL MASCOT
Answer: This gives a miser a warm feeling—COLD CASH

134. **Jumbles:** NOISY HURRY THRUSH AGENDA
Answer: How the passengers felt when their late flight ran out of drinks—HIGH AND DRY

135. **Jumbles:** BEFOG ENEMY FLATLY BARROW
Answer: What the weatherman longed for on a subzero night—A WARM FRONT

136. **Jumbles:** PRIZE QUOTA PYTHON PEPTIC
Answer: A citizen turns into this at tax time—A "PAY-TRIOT"

137. **Jumbles:** BIPED BALKY ZITHER DEBATE
Answer: This was drawn after her fast-paced dance scene—A DEEP BREATH

138. **Jumbles:** TWICE EXERT DIGEST ACHING
Answer: What the plumber did to his shoulder—"WRENCHED" IT

139. **Jumbles:** LOGIC FELON QUARTZ EXPEND
Answer: Letting his partner fall did this to their relationship—PUT IT ON ICE

140. **Jumbles:** RURAL FLORA CAMPUS LOUNGE
Answer: What the gossips enjoyed sharing at their lunch—RUMORS

141. **Jumbles:** DEMON HEFTY DIVIDE RAGLAN
Answer: When the novice went deep-sea diving, he discovered he was—IN OVER HIS HEAD

142. **Jumbles:** AGATE THINK NOBODY BLITHE
Answer: What the janitor did when the furnace failed—TOOK THE "HEAT"

143. **Jumbles:** PYLON KNAVE JOVIAL POMADE
Answer: Easy to get walking into a glass door—A PANE PAIN

144. **Jumbles:** JOUST MOTIF TREMOR ABACUS
Answer: What the hippie said when he went on an ocean cruise—"FAR OUT"

145. **Jumbles:** MUSIC ANNOY ANGINA PERMIT
Answer: What the candidates became when they joined the picnic race—RUNNING MATES

146. **Jumbles:** DECAY SURLY BEMOAN NAUSEA
Answer: What a steady income will let you keep—YOUR BALANCE

147. **Jumbles:** SYLPH LUSTY FEEBLE PERSON
Answer: A good thing for a tired witch to do—REST A "SPELL"

148. **Jumbles:** TWILL AWASH DRIVEL MOSAIC
Answer: Paying for a gourmet dinner can be this—HARD TO SWALLOW

149. **Jumbles:** SHINY BAKED EMBRYO JUMBLE
Answer: Why the math student couldn't fool the instructor—HE HAD HIS NUMBER

150. **Jumbles:** NOOSE PARTY FESTAL ORCHID
Answer: The transmission man was fired because he was—TOO "SHIFTY"

151. **Jumbles:** FLUID GAUZE DAMPEN WAYLAY
Answer: How the boss handled the heavy workload—HE "MANAGED"

152. **Jumbles:** PIVOT MOUNT NEGATE BANISH
Answer: What kind of case was it for the whodunit addict?—OPEN AND SHUT

153. **Jumbles:** BOGUS FOLIO JOYFUL SUBWAY
Answer: For a farmer, feeding the pigs is this—A "SWILL" JOB

154. **Jumbles:** FRIAR CHESS THORAX SEETHE
Answer: Tough to get out of a slow horse—FAST CASH

155. **Jumbles:** EIGHT GAUGE PEOPLE BISECT
Answer: A speedy way to build a staircase—STEP IT UP

156. **Jumbles:** VIXEN SHYLY ALPACA SYMBOL
Answer: What the "well-dressed" gentleman with scuffed shoes lacked—POLISH

157. **Jumbles:** TASTY DITTY HAZARD EVOLVE
Answer: Forty Degrees warmer than forecast put the weatherman here—THE "HOT" SEAT

158. **Jumbles:** IRATE AHEAD YEARLY MISFIT
Answer: Why Grandma put up pickles every year—SHE RELISHED IT

159. **Jumbles:** BILGE DUNCE HOOKUP PICNIC
Answer: What the coach enjoyed with his morning coffee—DUNKING

160. **Jumbles:** PRIOR OBESE VOLUME DISARM
Answer: The printer got a raise because his work was this—IMPRESSIVE

161. **Jumbles:** CORNER WEASEL ABRUPT PURIFY KINGLY GRASSY
Answer: What the doctor resorted to when the credit charges got too high—"PLASTIC" SURGERY

162. **Jumbles:** LAWFUL UNLOCK TUXEDO BOBBIN GOPHER PARLOR
Answer: The tailor had trouble with the wrestler because he was—TOUGH TO PIN DOWN

163. **Jumbles:** BECALM MORGUE AWHILE FRACAS PILLAR BEGONE
Answer: The ventriloquist said his dummy was this—A FIGURE OF "SPEECH"

164. **Jumbles:** BUTTON IMBUED RENEGE MYRIAD SHERRY MARLIN
Answer: The office worker yearned for a day at the beach because she had—A "BURNING" DESIRE

165. **Jumbles:** BENUMB UNTRUE ZENITH MEMOIR LEGUME STODGY
Answer: How did the tailors settle their differences?—"IRONED" THEM OUT

166. **Jumbles:** HOMAGE LARYNX GRATIS PAUNCH BELIEF MILDEW
Answer: What Mom became when she polished the silverware—A "SHINING" EXAMPLE

167. **Jumbles:** EMPLOY OXYGEN PRISON TROUGH COMPEL FILLET
Answer: When his prose brought tears to her eyes, she said it was—POETRY EMOTION

168. **Jumbles:** HAWKER BUCKLE ACCEDE VIABLE DOUBLY TOFFEE
Answer: Where the sailor ended up when he failed the exam—BELOW "C" LEVEL

169. **Jumbles:** ROBBER TRUISM BECAME CEMENT POCKET BEACON
Answer: Selling footstools turned into this—AN OTTOMAN EMPIRE

170. **Jumbles:** TYPHUS GRISLY PESTLE KIDNAP MEASLY DRAGON
Answer: Why did the misguided poet turn to crime?—RHYME DOESN'T PAY

171. **Jumbles:** BUNKER FIASCO PARISH JOYOUS FROSTY CHUBBY
Answer: What he needed when he got the bill for the car repairs—A SHOCK ABSORBER

172. **Jumbles:** BUBBLE HELPER MEADOW ARMADA JERSEY FLEECE
Answer: What he became when he bought the tire business—A "WHEELER" DEALER

173. **Jumbles:** HUNTER PACKET NUTRIA OUTCRY EMPIRE PILFER
Answer: The photographer won the award because his work was—PICTURE PERFECT

174. **Jumbles:** STYLUS PHYSIC BUREAU BANANA CRAYON TURGID
Answer: What he ended up with when he bought the stereo on sale—A "SOUND" PURCHASE

175. **Jumbles:** INNING AFFIRM HARBOR HAMPER GUITAR MALTED
Answer: What her bridge partner became when she won the bid—A "RIGHT HAND" MAN

176. **Jumbles:** BRANCH NOODLE WINTRY CAUGHT AWEIGH NEARBY
Answer: When the critics panned the tornado movie, it was—GONE WITH THE WIND

177. **Jumbles:** ICEBOX ABSORB FEUDAL HUMBLE FICKLE SURETY
Answer: What the student orchestra ended up playing—MUSICAL CHAIRS

178. **Jumbles:** BOUNTY COBALT ROSARY BEYOND CAVORT ABOUND
Answer: Junior stopped playing with the marionette because he—COULDN'T "STAND" IT

179. **Jumbles:** GOODLY BEHELD HOTBED MOTION ROTATE BURIAL
Answer: What Mom did when the kids got rowdy in the air—"GROUNDED" THEM

180. **Jumbles:** ANEMIA FUSION MEDLEY CAJOLE MUSTER SONATA
Answer: Enjoyed by the jazz quartet when the club was sold out—A "JAMMED" SESSION

Need More Jumbles®?

Order any of these books through your bookseller or call Triumph Books toll-free at 800-335-5323.

Jumble® Books

More than 175 puzzles each!

Animal Jumble®
$9.95 • ISBN: 1-57243-197-0

Jammin' Jumble®
$9.95 • ISBN: 1-57243-844-4

Jazzy Jumble®
$9.95 • ISBN: 978-1-57243-962-7

Jumble® at Work
$9.95 • ISBN: 1-57243-147-4

Joyful Jumble®
$9.95 • ISBN: 978-1-60078-079-0

Jumble® Explosion
$9.95 • ISBN: 978-1-60078-078-3

Jumble® Fever
$9.95 • ISBN: 1-57243-593-3

Jumble® Fiesta
$9.95 • ISBN: 1-57243-626-3

Jumble® Fun
$9.95 • ISBN: 1-57243-379-5

Jumble® Genius
$9.95 • ISBN: 1-57243-896-7

Jumble® Grab Bag
$9.95 • ISBN: 1-57243-273-X

Jumble® Jackpot
$9.95 • ISBN: 1-57243-897-5

Jumble® Jamboree
$9.95 • ISBN: 1-57243-696-4

Jumble® Jubilee
$9.95 • ISBN: 1-57243-231-4

Jumble® Juggernaut
$9.95 • ISBN: 978-1-60078-026-4

Jumble® Junction
$9.95 • ISBN: 1-57243-380-9

Jumble® Jungle
$9.95 • ISBN: 978-1-57243-961-0

Jumble® Madness
$9.95 • ISBN: 1-892049-24-4

Jumble® Mania
$9.95 • ISBN: 1-57243-697-2

Jumble® See & Search
$9.95 • ISBN: 1-57243-549-6

Jumble® See & Search 2
$9.95 • ISBN: 1-57243-734-0

Jumble® Surprise
$9.95 • ISBN: 1-57243-320-5

Jumble® Junction
$9.95 • ISBN: 1-57243-380-9

Jumpin' Jumble®
$9.95 • ISBN: 978-1-60078-027-1

Sports Jumble®
$9.95 • ISBN: 1-57243-113-X

Summer Fun Jumble®
$9.95 • ISBN: 1-57243-114-8

Travel Jumble®
$9.95 • ISBN: 1-57243-198-9

TV Jumble®
$9.95 • ISBN: 1-57243-461-9

Oversize Jumble® Books

More than 500 puzzles each!

Colossal Jumble®
$19.95 • ISBN: 1-57243-490-2

Generous Jumble®
$19.95 • ISBN: 1-57243-385-X

Giant Jumble®
$19.95 • ISBN: 1-57243-349-3

Gigantic Jumble®
$19.95 • ISBN: 1-57243-426-0

Jumbo Jumble®
$19.95 • ISBN: 1-57243-314-0

The Very Best of Jumble® BrainBusters
$19.95 • ISBN: 1-57243-845-2

Jumble® Crosswords™

More than 175 puzzles each!

Jumble® Crosswords™
$9.95 • ISBN: 1-57243-347-7

More Jumble® Crosswords™
$9.95 • ISBN: 1-57243-386-8

Jumble® Crosswords™ Adventure
$9.95 • ISBN: 1-57243-462-7

Jumble® Crosswords™ Challenge
$9.95 • ISBN: 1-57243-423-6

Jumble® Crosswords™ Jackpot
$9.95 • ISBN: 1-57243-615-8

Jumble® Crosswords™ Jamboree
$9.95 • ISBN: 1-57243-787-1

Jumble® BrainBusters™

More than 175 puzzles each!

Jumble® BrainBusters™
$9.95 • ISBN: 1-892049-28-7

Jumble® BrainBusters™ II
$9.95 • ISBN: 1-57243-424-4

Jumble® BrainBusters™ III
$9.95 • ISBN: 1-57243-463-5

Jumble® BrainBusters™ IV
$9.95 • ISBN: 1-57243-489-9

Jumble® BrainBusters™ 5
$9.95 • ISBN: 1-57243-548-8

Hollywood Jumble® BrainBusters™
$9.95 • ISBN: 1-57243-594-1

Jumble® BrainBusters™ Bonanza
$9.95 • ISBN: 1-57243-616-6

Boggle™ BrainBusters™
$9.95 • ISBN: 1-57243-592-5

Boggle™ BrainBusters™ 2
$9.95 • ISBN: 1-57243-788-X

Jumble® BrainBusters™ Junior
$9.95 • ISBN: 1-892049-29-5

Jumble® BrainBusters™ Junior II
$9.95 • ISBN: 1-57243-425-2

Fun in the Sun with Jumble® BrainBusters™
$9.95 • ISBN: 1-57243-733-2